D0994176

Health, Lifestyle
and Environment

Health, Lifestyle and Environment: Countering the Panic

British Library Cataloguing in Publication Data

Health, lifestyle and environment : countering
the panic.
304.2

ISBN 0907631444

Published in North America by
Manhattan Institute and in the UK by
The Social Affairs Unit.
Book production by Crowley Esmonde Ltd.
Typeset in Times by Harrison Typesetting,
Whitton, Middlesex.
Printed and bound in Great Britain by
SRP Ltd, Exeter.

Contents

The authors

Dr Digby Anderson is Director of the Social Affairs Unit in London. He holds a PhD in sociology and is a member of the UK Economic and Social Research Council. His publications include *Health Education in Practice, Full Circle: Bringing up Children in the Post Permissive Society, A Diet of Reason: Sense and Nonsense in the Healthy Eating Debate, Drinking to Your Health: the allegations and the evidence* and *The Megaphone Solution: government attempts to cure social problems with mass media campaigns.* He is a contributor to the London *Spectator, The Times,* and the *Daily* and *Sunday Telegraph.*

Professor Peter Berger is Professor of Sociology at Boston University, having been on the faculty since 1981. He has also taught at the University of North Carolina, Rutgers University, the New School for Social Research and the Hartford Theological Seminary. He is the author of 12 books, including *The Social Construction of Reality, The Heretical Imperative* and *The Capitalist Revolution.* He holds a PhD from the New School for Social Research and an LLD from Loyola University.

Robert Browning is an International Business Consultant in Melbourne, Australia. A writer and former analyst for the Australian government, he has authored several reports dealing with international consumer and health issues. His most recent publication is *The Network: A Guide to Anti-Business Pressure Groups.*

Professor Peter Finch is Foundation Professor of Statistics at Monash University, Australia. Educated in Britain, he has published widely in academic journals. His areas of specialisation include statistical methodology and the analysis of health statistics.

Professor Raymond Johnstone is a Fellow of the University of Western Australia and a former Senior Research Fellow with Australia's Health and Medical Research Council. His research specialisms are neurophysiology and public health. His books include *Health Scare: The Misuse of Public Health Policy* (with C Ulyatt). He holds a PhD in physiology from Monash University.

Irving Kristol is Senior Fellow at the American Enterprise Institute. His books include *Two Cheers for Capitalism, On the Democratic Idea in America* and *The Crisis in Economic Theory* (with Nathan Glazer). He has been co-editor of *The Public Interest* since 1965. He served on the faculty of New York University from 1968 to 1988 and was appointed the John M Olin Professor of Social Thought in 1979. He is a member of the *Wall Street Journal's* 'Board of Contributors'. He is a graduate of the City College of New York.

Dr James Le Fanu MD is a general practitioner in London and medical columnist of *The Sunday Telegraph*. He is the author of *Eat Your Heart Out* and *Healthwise: The Essential Guide for the Over 60s*. He is a graduate of Cambridge University.

Mark Mills is Executive Director of the Center for Science, Technology and Media in Washington DC. A physicist with a degree from Queen's University in Canada, he holds several patents in the fields of integrated circuits, fibre optics, defence and solid state devices. He has served as consultant to the White House Office of Technology Policy and the Congressional Office of Technology Assessment. He is founding partner of Science Concepts Inc, a research-consulting firm in energy and environmental economics and regulation.

Dr Petr Skrabanek MD, PhD is Reader in Community Health at Trinity College, Dublin. A specialist in epidemiology and the sociology of medicine, he is co-author of *Follies and Fallacies in Medicine* (with James McCormack, President of the Irish College of General Practitioners).

Professor Aaron Wildavsky is Professor of Political Science at the University of California at Berkeley. Major works include *The Politics of the Budgetary Process* and *Risk and Culture* (with Mary Douglas). He serves on the editorial board of *Policy Sciences, Journal of Public Policy* and the *Journal of Public Administration* and is a member of the Research and Development Strategies Panel at the National Research Council. He is an associate at the Survey Research Center at the University of California and holds a PhD from Yale University.

1 Introduction and Summary

The Harvard Club Conference

In the summer of this year, distinguished scholars representing different sciences and social sciences and from the US, Europe and Australasia, participated in a symposium at the Harvard Club. The topic of the symposium, sponsored by the London based Social Affairs Unit and New York's Manhattan Institute for Public Policy Research was the 'new public health debate' about health, lifestyle and environment. This book is an edited version of their contributions.

The Nub of the Issue: why are the healthiest, longest lived nations on earth so panicked about their health?

The central paradox of the new concern - sometimes panic - about threats to health can be stated quite simply. Why are the healthiest, longest lived societies the world has ever seen so concerned about their health? Why, for instance do Americans and the British who both have a wonderful range and ample quantity of good things to eat - at least in comparison with their African cousins - imagine they have a diet problem? The vast majority of both these populations drink beer, wines and spirits sensibly and thoroughly enjoy themselves doing so. Yet they are easily, if temporarily convinced by activists alleging that drink is a major, nationwide problem.

Why this largely unnecessary panic? The answers the authors give follow three broad themes. First, those promoting the concerns or indulging in them are not primarily moved by facts but either by self-interest or a *religious* impulse. Health is the new activism of the new class or the new religion. Second, the panic is due to the problems of presenting scientific research with all its nuances to a blip-attentive public and via a sensationalist media, neither of which know or are interested in knowing much science. Both media and public are impatient with uncertainty and caveats. This provides considerable scope for special interest groups and others to

7

provide and get away with dramatic 'findings' and panics. Third, and this is really an extension of the second, the whole concept of risk, be it about health or the environment, offers special difficulties and opportunities for exploitation in the public and political arena.

The nature of public health scares

It is said, on allegedly scientific grounds, that the modern Western lifestyle is uniquely unhealthy. It is said further that unless there is change - either by voluntary or by coercive means - the rates of premature death from degenerative illnesses will continue to rise. On why these illnesses have grown so common, opinion may seem divided. Some commentators emphasize lifestyle: what we eat, drink and smoke; others emphasize environment, the dangers from waste disposal, nuclear installations, polluted seas or rivers. Superficially the two are very different. The first appears to locate the trouble in what consumers choose to do and thus makes it their responsibility. The second suggests that risk is imposed on them by forces outside their control, largely corporations.

In practice, they are often very similar. It is an easy manoeuvre for the activists to portray the consumer's problems as ones forced on him by aggressive advertisers or producers. Not his fault if he smokes or hers if she is obese but that of the corporations. Both, too, find another common enemy in technology and economic growth. And both call for much the same answer, not more personal responsibility but government regulation. On where the final blame is to rest there is little dissent among the activists. In an unregulated market economy, they agree, consumer safety takes second place behind the quest for profit. Whether for marketing unhealthy products, or for poisoning the earth, air and water with their waste, businessmen are regarded as the main villains. The chief proposed cure is government intervention in one form or another. In the United States this has meant legislation which permits extensive powers for consumers to blame producers and exact large sums from them. In Europe it shows itself in calls for extra taxes or advertising bans on goods decreed to be 'unhealthy'.

Both the arguments that modern societies have high health risks and those which suggest regulation is the automatic answer are

8

widely accepted. But both are challenged in this book. There is little cause for believing that Westerners are uniquely unhealthy. They appear instead to be the healthiest people who ever lived, as has already been noted. No longer need they fear plague and famine. They are not infested with parasites. Their teeth are sound, their bodies large and strong. Almost invariably, they survive their infancy, and, overwhelmingly, their youth and middle age. The diseases that remain and kill, cancers and heart disease, are largely diseases of comparatively old age. Though they may be responsible for loss of lots of lives, they are not responsible for loss of many years of life. In short, all the great scourges of the past have been overcome. They have been overcome, moreover, through the rise of industrial capitalism. No other economic system has yet been shown to produce comparable rises in the standard of living, and hence of health and life expectancy. Wherever the coordinating role of market pricing has been rejected, living standards have at best crept forward. Often, they have declined.

Of course, it may be that scientific and industrial progress has raised problems as well as solved them. It is perfectly conceivable, for example, that a diet which has eliminated rickets also contributes to heart disease. But these problems can be investigated by scientific methods and, where necessary, solved by further scientific progress. Science, after all, is not a religion: it offers no body of final, revealed truth. It is a set of rules according to which statements about the world are tolerated or rejected. If certain such statements are found, on further investigation, to be partly untrue, better ones must be set in their place. It surely makes little sense to denounce the entire process, and put faith instead in what Robert Browning, a former Australian government analyst calls, in his chapter, 'strong new secular religions whose characteristics include opposition to economic growth, industrial technology and competitive capitalism'.

Yet, while perhaps unreasonable, this preference can be understood. Fear and ignorance - little though people like confessing to them - have always worked powerfully on the human mind, and have always been exploited by those able and willing to do so. Given the circumstances now prevailing throughout most of the West, there is nothing mysterious about the success enjoyed by the

9

spreaders or users of scares about public health - or, to give them a more compact term, the 'health activists'. It should be seen as no more than a new variation on an old theme.

Fear of death

Timor mortis me conturbat - the fear of death fills me with anxiety. Professor Peter Berger of Boston University quotes this line from a mediaeval hymn as exactly describing the 'cultural climate of pervasive anxiety' that he sees about him. As the immediate fear of death has diminished in the West, so has its general fear increased. He gives two causes. First, people today are no longer accustomed from an early age to the presence of death and suffering.

> Who has seen a corpse in Western society before I don't know what age? We certainly don't see many lepers. Serious illness is tucked away. So, we live in an extremely sheltered world and as a result we are coddled in an unprecedented way in terms of human history. Psychologists should not be surprised that we become very fearful.

Second, medical progress appears to be on the brink of offering large, if not yet permanent, extensions to life expectancy. For obvious reasons, people think it hard that they might not live long enough to take advantage of this offer. Add a general inclination to look to the government as protector and benefactor, and the first requirement for health activism to flourish is met. Just hint a danger in something - that it is a carcinogen, or damaging to the heart, or whatever - and the Western public will fall into a state of hypochondriacal terror, and will look to the government for action.

Ignorance about science

Add also to this an inability to assess the worth of such hints. The ability to do so would require an understanding of scientific fact and reasoning that is for the most part absent. Not only the general public, but also the well-educated and those who determine the content of the media, have the greatest difficulty assessing the worth of scientific - and not so scientific - claims. According to Mark Mills, Executive Director of the Center for Science, Technology and Media in Washington DC:

> About 60 per cent of the American population believe that dinosaurs and people lived at the same time. About half the population do not know that an electron is much smaller than an atom. About one fourth of the population does not know that the earth orbits the sun; half the population does not know how long it takes the earth to go around the sun.

People believe in the most improbable things - in 'lucky numbers', in the paranormal, in flying saucers, in anything wonderful and capable of arousing lively passions. When told that something is bad for their health, they scarcely ever ask how bad, but pass straight on to considering what action to take or demand to be taken. There was, for example, a certain risk involved in living next door to Three Mile Island during the whole course of the nuclear failure there. This was cried up in all the media as something almost unprecedentedly horrible, and was generally accepted as such. Yet the statistical risk of death was exactly the same as a canoeist runs every six minutes. Perhaps people fear cancer more than they do drowning. Certainly, few paused in 1980 to compare the various risks.

What motivates the activists?

There is no single group of beneficiaries from the modern health panic. It can be turned to the support of so many interests, sometimes acting in concert, sometimes against each other. But these do seem to fall under two broad headings. First, there are the medical puritans, or those haunted by what H L Mencken called the 'fear that someone, somewhere, may be happy'. Few nowadays suggest pleasure is evil or put linen drapes around table legs. But the underlying substance of puritanism remains the same in every generation: what changes is the form. Professor J R Johnstone of the University of Western Australia finds it sad but amusing to draw out the continuities. There has always been a minority of doctors and medical campaigners ready to condemn pleasure as unhealthy. A century ago, they made the world unhappy by dwelling on the alleged horrors of 'solitary vice' - how it could bring on every condition from catarrh to insanity. Today, with God and the old morality out of fashion, they find new means of making the blood run cold.

11

Accordingly, they declaim against smoking and drinking and eating too heartily, passing on every fact and half-fact that comes their way.

Second, there is what has been called the New Class. In every Western country, to a greater or less degree, there is now a large section of the middle class for whom money, though still important, is desired far less ardently than power. Admittedly, as Professor Irving Kristol, Senior Fellow at the American Enterprise Institute, observes, there have always been such people. The difference is that, in the past, they contrived to make themselves useful - by joining the armed forces, or going out and ruling an empire. Today, these options are closed, and it is their fellow citizens on whom they must in some way impose themselves. Kristol explains:

> They do want to "participate". And they're clever enough to know that they are a minority, so there's no point in their getting directly involved in politics for the most part. Some do, but most of them do not. That would not be a very smart thing to do: they could lose an election. What they have done is engage in what a Marxist called ...the "march through the institutions".

They begin with the universities, but then spread to journalism, to law and to the higher reaches of the civil service and other organs of administration. To assist them in this, they need a justifying ideology – something that is at once likely to prove generally popular and to enlarge the size and prestige of such institutions as they have made their own.

The articulation of health scares is exactly this. It allows its advocates to announce themselves to be working solely for the public interest. It impresses the public. Above all, it impresses the politicians. At a time of escalating health budgets, any concentration on prevention as opposed to cure is likely to be welcome. And, to quote Robert Browning again,

> [i]f there is one universal theme in worldwide public interest health campaigns which distinguishes them from conventional health care campaigns, it is the almost total emphasis on what they call preventive rather than curative action. The official slogan of the World Health Organisation is now the somewhat utopian "Health for

12

All by the Year 2000".

He notes the increasing tendency of economists, sociologists and lawyers to determine health policy rather than doctors. He notes also the linked tendency to replace the sober and detached language traditionally associated with scientific reasoning with a strident activism. The declared ends of this 'advocacy science' is less the advancement of knowledge than a heavier weight of controls on what can be produced or sold. After an examination of the main American campaigning bodies, he concludes ominously:

> They want (perhaps demand is a better word) to see the traditional separation of church and state reversed and their values established as official state ideology. Opposition views and lifestyles are seen as sinful. Many have no use for the tolerance that has been a keystone of liberal democratic societies.

The sincerity of much health activism

It must not, however, be assumed that self-interest is by itself the key to understanding the health activists. They are also idealists. Just because they happen to benefit the most - or even exclusively - from health and environmental programmes does not prevent them from from believing in their own absolute rightness. They are the products of the anti-materialist youth culture of the 1960s and 1970s. They have never wanted for anything, and so have never seen fit to praise or even appreciate the wonders of universal affluence. As Professor Kristol observes, they are drenched in the intellectual and ideological impulses, the anti-capitalist, anti-bourgeois, anti-modern impulses of the 19th and early 20th centuries. While they use rational means, their ends really are as mystical and neo-pagan as they can often be brought to confess. It really is to them an article of faith that progress is bad for humanity and for the environment which sustains us. If they were just cynical manipulators, their power would be all extension and no base. Their strength - and, thus, their danger - lies in their utter sincerity.

13

Valuable health education distinguished from suspect health activism

Nor is every attempt at public health education to be condemned as the advancing of sectional interest. Dr Digby Anderson, Director of the London-based Social Affairs Unit, distinguishes between sensible, modest health education based on sound science, and ambitious government intervention precipitated by scare headlines. The essential criterion is whether or not the educators offer their lessons or seek to impose them when the public chooses to ignore them. He sees true health education as

> families, intermediate community agencies and schools giving children at school information about behaviour-related diseases, encouraging them to think about the values involved in approving or rejecting certain behaviour and developing their capacity to take decisions and the responsibility for them. In the health care field, it means helping doctors and others to communicate effectively with their patients in the treatment of actual illnesses and in warning of conditions at risk. But most important of all, health education also occurs spontaneously when there is free public debate about health and behaviour.

Dr Anderson distinguishes between educators who accept that they are dealing with free and responsible beings and the sort of activism which cries for legal and administrative controls, and a monopoly of information. As a typical instance of coercive education, he draws attention to the health report leaked to the press in the UK in May 1991. Described by the Health Minister presenting it as 'the most comprehensive of its kind in the world', this sets various targets to be achieved before the end of the century. There is, for example, to be a 30 per cent reduction in coronary heart disease. Fewer cigarettes are to be smoked. Fewer fatty and other disfavoured sorts of food are to be eaten. All this to be achieved by mass publicity campaigns, and by regulation. The Report lays down specific recommendations of how many calories and nutrients are required, taking into account age, sex and other variables. The Health Education Authority has been asked to simplify these recommendations into healthy eating guides, and even a cookery book. The Government is also to campaign for new European Community regulations on food labelling so that consumers may be better informed on what their food contains.

But what if the millions of individuals concerned decide not to change their behaviour? How can the Minister set targets when it is individuals who make the decisions? Either he is simply saying what he would like them to decide or something more coercive is envisaged. It is reminiscent of a state plan: indeed it is a state plan with all the weaknesses that we now know characterises them. Most do not come true and most are coercive.

One way of achieving compliance to mass health goals is regulation. Two examples proposed by the activists are food labelling and the banning or regulation of advertising of 'unhealthy goods'. There is no end to the messages activists of all sorts - not just health -would like to be printed on labels. Given their way, they would require the disclosure of so much information that an encyclopaedia rather than a label would need to be fixed to every product. This would tell the consumer, among much else - what the ingredients were; which were in the slightest degree dangerous, and to what extent; which were 'natural', and what was meant by the description as such; whether the product had been tested on animals, and, if so, under what conditions; how comparable it was, in weight, size, concentration, and so forth, to other similar products; whether the manufacturer had investments or any other connection with certain unpopular countries; and the list would continue further.

The control of advertising was not mentioned in the Report, but is advocated by many of the health activists who assisted in its preparation. This, even if it were likely to achieve its stated goal - of allowing only truthful claims - would be objectionable. In fact the scientific truth is rarely pure and never simple and the whole truth cannot be fitted into a brief advertisement. Advertising bans and rigid controls would also reduce the independence and diversity of the media, by diminishing the revenue now raised from advertisers. And restrictions on commercial speech would set a ready precedent for government interference in other forms of speech.

About even the first means advocated in the Report, mass publicity campaigns, Dr Anderson is doubtful. These are bound to be inefficient. They cannot take account of the immense diversity of consumers. Different people have different health needs and different pleasures. Advice suitable for some is not suitable for all. Those who cannot handle alcohol are unlikely to be helped by campaigns that treat all, including the moderate majority, as prospective alcoholics.

What, moreover, if millions of British consumers prefer to ignore the recommendations? Suppose as much sugar is eaten as before, and as many cigarettes smoked - how then are the health targets to be achieved? 'Either the target is a pious and empty hope or it is indeed coercive', Dr Anderson says. Real health education is a blessing, but, in common with any other search for the truth, it requires debate and a diversity of views. Much of what passes nowadays for health education is at best a parody. It has various truer descriptions - paternalism, nannyism, consumer-socialism, even food Leninism. But, whatever it may be called, it must not be confused with legitimate education.

The use and abuse of science

The centre of the debate about health panics is the use and misuse of science for it is 'scientific findings' which the activists use to scare the public and push governments into regulation. The main source of scientific support is a debased epidemiology. Before about 1950, epidemiology was largely a matter of studying the patterns of infectious diseases. Given careful observation and interpretation, solid, and often spectacular, results were possible. But the elimination of most infections has required the epidemiologists to find some new activity. Professor Petr Skrabanek of Trinity College, Dublin, describes how they have turned instead to looking for associations between the principal modern killers - heart disease and cancer - and some particular behaviour or mode of living.

Unfortunately, these associations are nearly always ambiguous. In the last century, it was a simple matter of observation to trace the spread of cholera in London's East End to a single water pump. It is a far harder matter to trace some degenerative illness back to any of the risk factors now studied -

> either personal characteristics (age, sex, weight, height, diet, habits, customs, vices) or situational characteristics

16

(geography, occupation, environment, air, water, sun, gross national product, stress, density of doctors).

Even where not based on wishful thinking or statistical incompetence, the claims now most often made can indicate risks too small to worry about.

As might be expected, given that there are so many epidemiologists, all doing the same sort of thing, their advice can on the whole be confusing. Thus, depending on who is currently speaking, it is said - that a third of all cancers are caused by diet, and that 70 per cent are so caused; that coffee makes women both sexually inactive and sexually active, and that it causes and does not cause heart disease; we are urged to drink decaffeinated coffee to be on the safe side, and then warned that one of the chemicals used in decaffeination causes cancer. The warnings come thick and fast, without regard to consistency. At the last count, there were 246 risk factors identified for coronary heart disease alone.

Uncertainty has not stopped the epidemiologists from lending their support to the health activists. With their blessing, lectures are given to the public on the evils of tobacco and alcohol and fatty foods. The claims are set before it in plain and lurid English. The ambiguities and reservations are left behind, in the better scientific journals.

Take, for example, the case for the existence of 'passive smoking'. This has been amazingly successful. In the early 1980s, Professor Berger attended an international conference on smoking and health. He was told by one of the anti-smoking activists of the goal to 'make smoking something that was done by consenting adults in private'. At the time, the anti-smoking cause was a minority concern. Today, and largely because of the fears raised by the various passive smoking claims, that goal has largely been reached.

Yet Professor Johnstone looks in some detail at the epidemiological evidence, and finds it at best 'circumstantial and incomplete'. One of the main studies cited is that of the Japanese researcher T Hirayama. He investigated the relative incidence of lung cancer in the non-smoking wives of smoking and non-smoking men, finding a higher incidence in the wives of the former. Since their publication in 1981, his findings have been one of the main supports of the campaign for restrictions on smoking in public and for higher taxes on tobacco. They have regularly been cited in the mass media as all the conclusive proof that could ever be required.

In fact, they were and are highly controversial and several scholars have pointed out defects in his work they consider substantial. Professor Johnstone lists the defects and controversies around Hirayama's work. But what is even more telling is the way this work has been used by activists who make no mention of such alleged defects and controversies. Professor Johnstone goes on to show the problems involved in 'adding up' a number of studies to reach an overall conclusion and challenges the supposed link between health and exercise.

To be sure, the health activists seldom tell outright lies. They more often present information in ways which must lead readers to jump to stronger conclusions than are justified. Peter Finch, from Monash University, Australia, examines this misleading use of statistics by the health activists. He shows how maximum response is ensured by the careful choice of language. Invariably, it is relative rather than absolute risk which is emphasised.

He looks at the case for passive smoking - not as made by Hirayama, but by the Independent Scientific Committee on Smoking and Health, the report of which was published by the British Government in 1988. It is claimed that the non-smoking wives of smoking men have a 30 per cent higher chance of contracting lung cancer than non-smoking wives of non-smoking husbands. Assuming its truth - undoubtedly a large assumption - this is alarming. 30 per cent sounds like an enormous increase in risk. Yet, looking at the basis of this claim, the increase is put in perspective. 'The annual death rate' says Professor Finch,

> from lung cancer among non-smoking wives of non-smoking men is of the order of 6 per 100,000. Among the non-smoking wives of smoking men the corresponding figure is 8 per 100,000. Thus 2 in every 99,994 non-smoking wives of smoking husbands die of lung cancer that, it is claimed, should be attributed to the effects of passive smoking. This is an exposure risk of almost 1 in 50,000, about the chance of tossing 16 heads in a row... the most that can be said about the alleged link between passive smoking and lung cancer is that if there is one, then it is so small that it is difficult to measure it accurately and the

risk, if any, is well below the level of those to which we pay attention.

Unfortunately, it is the alarming facts that are accepted. For, as said, most media consumers, indeed most media producers have little competence in scientific scrutiny and a considerable appetite for sensation. They are neither able to understand the ambiguities and reservations implicit in what the health activists tell them, nor often willing to try to understand them. By not objecting to the distortions made by the health activists - by going so far as to sanction them - epidemiologists are contributing to an erosion of scientific standards among themselves and of rationality throughout society at large.

Particular campaigns: food

How full the Western diet is of poisons is a favourite theme of the health activists. Dr James Le Fanu, a medical columnist and general practitioner, doubts that it can be so deadly. 'If [it] has played an important role' he says,

> in prolonging...longevity (of which there can be no doubt) it cannot in the same breath be denounced as a cause of the age-related diseases that people die from as a consequence.

This, however, is the claim so often made. Heart disease is routinely attributed to the mass liking for fatty or sugary foods. It is the prevailing nutritional wisdom. He continues,

> Beliefs about the harmful nature of the Western diet have been around for the better part of twenty years. They have been endorsed by countless expert committees, are believed in and promoted by virtually every doctor, and in popular culture they have the same status of self evident veracity as the common belief that smoking is harmful to health.

Yet the claim rests on a very slender empirical base; and, until the 1960s, the exact opposite was believed with equal certainty. Since the studies of Sir John Boyd Orr in the 1930s, the orthodox view of a healthy diet had been one rich in fat, low in fibre. More animal protein was held to be the answer to all our nutritional problems. Bread and other high carbohydrate foods were despised as

19

empty calories. Now, this change of view stemmed from no corresponding fresh discovery in the science of nutrition. All the fundamentals had been discovered by the 1930s; and while our knowledge since then has deepened, it has not been revolutionised. What changes have occurred have been of fashion rather than of understanding.

It would, of course, be shocking had the nutritionists exchanged solid wisdom for the latest fashion. But this has not been the case. For it seems that the preceding faith in high fat products was no less fashionable in its turn, and no more justified by the evidence.

Much was said in the 1930s about a supposed crisis of malnutrition among the working classes. This, it was proclaimed by the scientific and political establishment, could only be ended by increasing their consumption of animal proteins. These claims were demonstrably untrue. Certainly, children in state schools tended to be smaller than those of the same age in the public schools, and this was attributable to differences in diet. But there was only a slightly higher incidence among the former of anaemia, rickets and the other diseases of malnourishment. Despite their supposedly poor diet, they were suffering no real ill-effects.

By the 1960s, fears of mass malnutrition had receded. Instead, the talk was of an immense rise in heart disease. This was linked to the consumption of animal proteins, and the old dietary campaign was thrown into reverse. Again, the evidence was far from certain. Dr Le Fanu draws attention, among much else, to the similar fat consumption of Americans and Swedes, and to their wholly different patterns of heart disease - and, very strangely, how Swedish immigrants soon conform to the American pattern even without varying the amount of fat consumed in their diet. The rise and subsequent fall in the incidence of heart disease among Westerners coincided with a rise and fall in the consumption of animal proteins, but to a wholly disproportionate extent. He concludes that

> coronary heart disease must primarily be an unexplained biological phenomenon in which fat consumption or a high cholesterol level (caused by defective genes) and cigarette smoking may have an additional but not determinant role.

Since the popularity, each in its time, of the two main sets of dietary guide-lines described above were due not to their solid establishment - for they had none - Dr Le Fanu traces them to more general movements of ideology. In the 1930s, depression and poverty were responded to with calls for the working classes to be allowed to share the eating habits of the upper classes. By the 1960s, the rising belief among part of the intellectual elite in the harmfulness of prosperity was reflected in calls for an ascetic diet. Both fashions relied 'on a partial presentation of facts that [struck] a chord with prevailing ideological beliefs'. The sort of evidential requirements normal in true science neither did nor do come into the matter.

Particular campaigns: the environment

But, of all the claims made by the health activists, none alarms more than those concerning the environment. When individuals are panicked into concern about butter or cigarettes, they can at least give these up and await the sensational improvements in health promised them by the health activists. What can be done, though, if the whole environment is believed to be dangerous? There is little room here for individual action. For the most part, the dangers cannot even be detected. Their effect is cumulative, and only becomes apparent when nothing can be done to avoid it. The best solution might seem to be a secular version of Pascal's wager. If the health activists are given into, freedom and economic growth will at the least be impaired: but life might continue. Ignore them, and there might be few left able to enjoy the fruits of unrestrained progress. Yet, once again, if looked at calmly and with all the relevant knowledge, the alarms often evaporate. Repeatedly, those who raise them show a disregard for scientific practices and a selective use of statistics that ought to be a source of shame to the intellectual leaders of a technological civilisation.

As an instance of this tendency, Professor Aaron Wildavsky of the University of California at Berkeley, looks at the Love Canal scandal of the late 1970s. This New York State housing development was found to have been sited near a chemical waste dump. The media were at once filled with allegations that the residents were afflicted with higher rates of Hodgkin's disease, rectal cancer and asthma. All the residents were bought out with public money. The Federal Superfund Program for cleaning up toxic waste

21

sites was a direct result of the incident.

But the studies on which these allegations were based were not at all rigorous. In one, a group of residents was invited to fill in a questionnaire about how unhealthy they felt: they were not medically examined; nor were their answers checked against those given by people living elsewhere. In any group of people, some will inevitably be ill. Given a large enough group, there will even be apparent clusters of illnesses. But a far wider and more sophisticated induction is required before any causal hypothesis can be raised on such evidence. In the Love Canal incident, no inductions made at the time had either width or sophistication. Subsequently, when proper studies were conducted, it was found impossible to prove that so much as a cold resulted from living near the chemical waste. None of the wastes was ever found in air or water samples. The houses are now being refurbished for new residents.

To digress somewhat, Mark Mills provides an amusing *reductio ad absurdum* of the health activist approach to statistics. A British statistical expert

> found clusters of a specific cancer in the vicinity of military installations. It turns out that the 'installations' were medieval castles ...[He] had simply searched for a disease that clustered around a selected set of physical locations.

To an unskilled researcher - or, perhaps, to a thoroughly skilled health activist - such 'factual illusions' are easy to create. They are released to a friendly or uncritical media, and are uncomprehendingly received by the public. The refutations come later. But, by then, the harm has been done, and attention has shifted to some new scare. After the Love Canal alarm had been quashed, for example, the Superfund Program continued, its budget now having risen from an initial half billion dollars to more than $10 billion. Much of this - as might be expected - goes on the salaries of the program's legal staff.

Wildavsky looks also at the campaign against Alar, a growth retardant used to increase orchard yields. The same kind of story emerges. After two decades of quiet success, the chemical was at last denounced by, among others, Ralph Nader and Meryl Streep as a carcinogen. Huge amounts of it had been given to laboratory animals, and they had then developed tumours. Figures were produced to show how many children could die each year from drinking apple juice containing it. There was a mass panic throughout the United States. The apple and apple juice markets collapsed as nervous parents stopped buying what might have been a poison. Eventually, after much campaigning, and further animal experiments, a Federal ban was imposed on its use.

Yet no evidence was ever produced to show that Alar definitely was a carcinogen. Even granting the claims that is was, one apple tainted with it would have had less than half the carcinogenic potency of a glass of chlorinated tap water. For a human being to absorb as much Alar as the unfortunate rodents had been given to eat, something like 19,000 bottles of apple juice would need to be drunk down at once. Compared with the natural poisons that plants develop as a protective - and which in many cases our own defences overcome - Alar was nothing. The panic was wholly unjustified. But, again, the harm has been done:

> Alar is still banned. Consumer confidence has been shaken. Apple growers have been harmed. All this has happened without either basic reasons in the science of the subject to believe the product was harmful or experimental evidence to that effect.

Wildavsky's judgement has been seconded by the British Government. When the panic crossed the Atlantic, the Advisory Committee on Pesticides was instructed to examine the arguments against Alar. Its conclusion was that '[e]ven for children consuming the maximum quantities of apples and apple juice, subjected to the maximum treatment with daminozide, there is no risk'.

The same deflationary analysis is applied to claims about Somatotropin, asbestos and Agent Orange. In every case, Wildavsky finds the same pattern of exaggerated or unfounded allegations of harm, the same calls for government regulation - or, at any rate, the spending of government money. He sees an entire movement of 'progressive scientists' and their allies, dedicated to showing how what they call corporate greed is subjecting ordinary people to unjustified risks of painful or fatal illnesses. Anyone who dares question their findings or methodology is denounced as an apologist for big business.

Conclusion

The case presented in this book, then, is that people are easily panicked where life and health are concerned; that they know too little about the relevant sciences to assess what they are told; that they are exploited by sectional interest groups; that science itself is perverted, or its findings misrepresented, in the generation of health scares. These are the problems identified. Are any answers suggested?

The authors suggest none in the short term. In the longer term, much is to be hoped. There is a natural bias in the human mind towards the truth of any matter. The sort of future offered by the health activists - which, looked at closely, shows itself as no more than a return to the poverty and wretchedness of the past - is flatly at variance with what most people appear really to want. The time will almost certainly come when scientific truth and calm humanity are again the established guides.

That, however, is in the long term. For the moment, the health activists must have their day. As Professor Kristol concludes,

we have some deep problems. It's not just a question of educating the people: who's going to do the educating? We can educate a few, but since they [the new class including the health activists] control the universities - by now, the high schools as well - it's not so easy to educate large numbers of people. I think we are fighting a defensive action, a holding action. Our advantage is that they cannot succeed in governing in a way to satisfy ordinary men and women...On the other hand, there they are. The laws have been passed, the institutions set up, the rules made: and I think our experience of the past ten years under quite conservative administrations indicates the difficulty of rolling back the wave.

2 Towards a Religion of Health Activism

Peter Berger

Health has become a source of paranoia

Recently, in a novel by John Mortimer, I read a statement that I find very congenial - namely, that one of the great advantages of social change is how it reconciles one to one's own mortality. I find this also a very plausible statement. Hypochondria and paranoia, which have always been inflictions of individuals, have now become very firmly institutionalized in most Western societies, and especially in the United States, which is in the lead of this cultural change - indeed, of most cultural changes. It is not a pleasant prospect.

The politics of health is a subject with vast ramifications, and there are complex medical and economic issues involved which I am completely incompetent to discuss. Instead, I will comment on what I think is the social and cultural context of these issues. Essentially, I will present a simple thesis - that health has become a sort of religion in the advanced industrial societies of the West, and that the United States is clearly in the lead.

Now, it seems to me that there is an interesting paradox here if we look at our societies historically. Today, in the West, we enjoy longer lives, better health and safety than human beings have ever enjoyed before. At the same time, we have a cultural climate of pervasive anxiety.

The less people see of suffering, the more they fear it

Yet, while this seems a paradox, if we look at it psychologically, it is not really so mysterious. It is the coddled child that is the most frightened when confronted with those realities against which no coddling is possible. Certainly, our children are very coddled indeed.

I have often been struck by that fact. I recall the legend of the Buddha's childhood. Named Gautama, he was the son of a prince who, for reasons connected with a prophecy, tried to shield him from any sight of human suffering. This must have been quite a job in the India of the 6th century BC. Then, as a young man, on a single day, he had three visions of human suffering - an old man, a leper, and finally a corpse being taken out to cremation. These shocked him so much that he decided to leave the palace and seek enlightenment in the wilderness.

What struck me was that, while this must have been an extraordinarily difficult feat for Gautama's father, this is how our children grow up today. Who has seen a corpse in Western society before - I don't know what age? We certainly don't see many lepers. Serious illness is tucked away. So, we live in an extremely sheltered world, and as a result are coddled in an unprecedented way in terms of human history. Psychologists should not be surprised that we become so very fearful.

The anti-smoking movement: the paradigm of health activism

I give little time to particular questions of health or health movements, with the exception of the anti-smoking movement. In many ways, this is a paradigmatic case. It relates to a lot of other things in this society. In many ways, smoking is a window on the world. It touches on almost everything that happens.

One thing that is simply amazing to any observer of Western society is the incredible success of this movement - especially in the United States - over no more than about 15 years. Concern about smoking used to be roughly on the same level as fear of unidentified flying objects. It was a cause espoused by little sectarian groups jumping up and down.

Today, smoking in the United States has been put more or less where the anti-smokers wanted it put. Around 1980, I heard a spokesman for the anti-smoking movement say, at an international conference on smoking and health, that the purpose of his movement was to make smoking something that was done between consenting adults in private. This is about what it is in much of the United States today. His movement has scored an amazing success.

An outside observer would certainly ask how this is to be

explained. Why has the anti-smoking movement been so success-ful? I would suggest that an understanding of this particular case will be very helpful in understanding the wider phenomenon that interests me - the health cult, or health as a religion.

I immediately put aside as irrelevant what might be an obvious answer to the above question. It might seem commonsensical to call the anti-smoking phenomenon a rational response to a real threat; to say that there is a real threat, that people have become aware of it, and that they have stopped smoking themselves, and want others to join them.

I am not competent to judge the scientific evidence in this matter, but I doubt if many other people are either. As anyone knows who has examined the literature as a whole, rather than just the propaganda of the anti-smoking movement, the evidence is very complicated. It has mostly to do with extremely complex statistical reasoning which most other people as well as I are absolutely unable to understand.

What, then, is inevitably involved here is not how people re-spond to a certain body of evidence which they cannot evaluate, but how they put active faith in certain authorities who tell them that this evidence is conclusive.

Humanity ruled by vested interests and vested ideas

Most of these authorities are connected with government. What I find very intriguing as a sociologist is that many people who would not believe a word said, for example, by the United States Secretary of Defense take as gospel truth what is pronounced by the Secretary of Health and Human Services. This is not a rational response to a body of evidence. It is an act of faith. When people perform such acts, the reasonable question to ask is why they should do so.

The usual answer - at least from a social science point of view - is two-fold. The first, which is the kind of answer that economists like, is to see it as a rational choice: people act because it is in their interest to do so. The second answer is that people do not always follow their rational interest. Instead, they do what hangs together with other things that they believe in. An explanation in terms of vested interest is contrasted with another in terms of vested ideas.

When it comes to smoking - and, indeed, the whole area of health - I think we shall find both these explanations very useful.

There is now a network of powerful anti-smoking interests. Weighing these against the main vested interest on the other side, this being the tobacco industry (smokers in the main not being very well organised), I don't know how their respective strengths would be estimated. That is difficult to assess. But the picture emerging from the anti-smoking propaganda - one of upright citizens struggling against these powerful vested interests - is complete nonsense. There are powerful vested interests on both sides.

Aaron Wildavsky and I were associated some years ago with a study - he more than I - of the anti-smoking movement in the United States and the United Kingdom. The picture we found was of large and complicated networks of institutions. Some were indeed anti-smoking groups. Others were private and governmental bureaucracies that had a strong vested interest in pushing an anti-smoking agenda. I am quite sure that the same is true of other health issues. There is money. There is status. There is power for people who are associated with these networks.

The cultural imperialism of the health activists

My own work as a sociologist has been mostly concerned with modernisation and third world development. What I find absolutely fascinating is how this Western creation, which the health cult plainly is, is being exported to non-Western countries through the World Health Organisation and other agents of what I think one could, in a very non-Marxist but accurate way, describe as 'cultural imperialism'. The United States is an extremely imperialist nation culturally speaking. Feminism, environmentalism, or whatever - every ideology that develops in the United States is rapidly diffused to places like India or Central Africa by powerful agencies. What happens to these ideas when they arrive there is both interesting and much of the time very funny.

Anxiety now a vested idea in Western societies

But I leave it to my fellow contributors to this book to go into the details of these vested interests. I look instead at the vested ideas.

28

Negatively speaking, there is, I repeat, a pervasive anxiety and a need to propitiate this. I am reminded of this line from an old mediaeval hymn: *Timor mortis me conturbat* - the fear of death fills me with anxiety. This sums up an entire way of thought in most Western countries today.

There is a positive, inspiring side to this. There is the ideal of long-lasting, if not eternal, youth. If this ideal has not yet been realised, it is no longer a fantasy. It is, however, coupled with a political aspect - a considerable faith in government as the principal agency which is to protect us from danger, and to help realise the ideal.

Arguments for regulation need a third party victim

Some years ago, I made a prediction. I mention this with pride, since social scientists rarely make predictions that come true. I made it in a paper that I wrote when I first became interested in the politics of health. I said that the anti-smoking movement had a big problem, at least in the Western democracies. Even if smoking really were so harmful to smokers as was claimed, the natural response would be to call it a matter of individual choice and resist calls for regulation. 'If I want to kill myself' the answer would go, 'that's my business. The Government should protect others against me, but not me against myself'.

The only solution to this problem available to the anti-smoking movement, I said, would be for it to find - and this was my term - an 'innocent bystander'. I suggested that one means of doing this would be to convince people that they could be harmed by the smoking of others.

This is exactly what happened - and on the basis of scientific evidence which strikes even me, a non-natural scientist, as very dubious indeed.

The ideological function of this search for innocent bystanders has been crucial, and continues to be the major legitimation of all manner of laws and other regulations in this area.

The paradigm continually repeated

The larger cultural location of this particular case has to do, of course, with health in general. There are both ideological affinities and political linkages between the paradigmatic anti-smoking movement and other issues such as cholesterol, diet in general, and -in the United States - the fascinating and full-blown revival of the temperance movement. The alcohol industry is now a major target of the health activists.

Environmentalism is an integral part of this. It is not an accident that, very early on, we began to speak of a smoke-free environment. The positive image which is pushed here with health is a bucolic view of what I like to call (I'm Viennese, and therefore dislike fresh air!) the 'natural manure movement'. It involves happy peasants, jumping through the grass, and - of course - not smoking, but eating the right foods and looking after their general health.

Then there is consumerism. Here is a movement with very strong anti-corporate animus. They spend their time denouncing those corporations which are trying to poison us in various ways.

Now, the closest affinity that I can find in all this is with a primary utopian theme in modern Western societies which I would call religious. It is the utopia of a rationally planned life, both individually and collectively, in which the pursuit of happiness is ever more fully guaranteed. In a sense, it is a modernised version of one of humanity's oldest dreams. The quest of Gilgamesh for immortality is one of the early classical instances of this dream. 'I want to be young' we say, 'if not forever, then for as long as possible'. Much of this relates, I think, to secularisation, the transfer of religious values into secular discourse.

Are there policy implications to the above? I think not very many. Rational argument tends to be weak when it deals with powerful cultural forces. But, I think from a policy point of view, one can certainly say that it is better to be aware of this larger context than not to be aware of it. If we are concerned with policy, either by business organisations or by government, it is, I feel, good to know what we are up against.

3   Who Are the Health Activists?

Robert Browning

Health activism: grass roots movement or elitist preserve?

The intention of this chapter is to flag, rather than try to elaborate in the space available, a number of key aspects and analytical tools which it would seem necessary to include in any political assessment of health activism and its bottom-line impact on the economy and society.

First, we may need to reconsider whether, in fact, it is society that is obsessed with health and risk avoidance, or whether this should be more correctly attributed to certain elites. If elites, we should further ask whether elitist commitment to health campaigns springs only from altruism and pragmatic reformism. To what extent are vested interests and associated ideologies, pressure group organisations, and political parties involved? Genuine progress in health and safety knowledge and effective reform obviously is to be welcomed and supported. But we must distinguish the positive aspects from any hijacking and misuse of health issues to advance special interest agendas likely to be counter-productive to declared public interest objectives.

Some years ago, Stanley Rothman and S Robert Lichter, under the auspices of the Research Institute at Columbia University, profiled the leaderships of several key institutions including not only the most influential media outlets in the United States, but also so-called public interest lobby groups. One way or another, almost all of these public interest groups are involved with health and risk campaigns, whether from consumer protection, environmentalist, public health and safety, or other such 'single issue' angles.

Rothman and Lichter concluded that there was a wide chasm between these elites and Middle America. Generally speaking the elites surveyed were, for example, overwhelmingly secular, affluent, and liberal (in the American sense, ie progressive); they believed business had too much influence on the nation, but that the media should have more.

Commenting on what he thought the survey told us about the public interest movement, Lichter said:

> Well, at its top it's primarily a movement of young lawyers...Young lawyers who were raised in comfortable circumstances, cosmopolitan environments, gravitated towards power centres of New York and Washington.
>
> As principal upholders of today's liberalism they represent an emerging political pattern...in their quest to represent the public interest, they obviously deviate quite often from the outlook and perspectives of the general public.

Lichter's comments back in 1983 are worth noting in relation to recent concern about the explosion of product litigation in the United States. This has created incentives both for consumers and lawyers to sue 'big business' and a community of interest between some lawyers and consumer activists.

Elites need 'victims' to 'protect'

Another influential observer to comment on the chasm between elites and ordinary folk is the best-selling author Tom Wolfe who coined such terms as 'radical chic'. In his book, *The Me Decade*, Wolfe wrote of the attraction which victims of society have for elites who aspire to the status and political influence of a protecting class. He believes that victims, especially of the Charlie Chaplin-figure type, helpless in the face of massive corporate and technological forces, have always been most appealing to certain sorts of intellectuals.

> These 'poor devils', Wolfe says in 'new journalist' style, so obviously need us [as their] Engineers of the Soul. We will pygmalionise this sad lump of clay into a homo novus, a New Man, with a new philosophy, new aesthe-tics, not to mention new Bauhaus housing and furniture.

Wolfe comments that, unfortunately for the social engineering elites, their potential victim constituency, ordinary folk, 'took the money and ran' as soon as capitalist society made its victims affluent. They left the nanny-staters holding their empty baby carriages.

Unfortunately, this was not the end of the story. Voluntary persuasion having failed, out-of-work protectors quickly counter-attacked. They set about building public policy apparatuses to harness powers of the state to force people to take the medicine they had chosen to refuse.

Vested interests and the New Class

Consequently, in scanning the public interest movement for vested interest, we need to look further than its association with plaintiff lawyers. We should also note theories of the New Class, or that section of the new knowledge class which, in Professor Peter Berger's words, 'depends directly or indirectly upon government subsidisation' and, accordingly, 'has a strong vested interest in the expansion of government services.'

Others have remarked on the extent to which the New Class seeks to utilise mechanisms of the Welfare State to consolidate and expand its position in society. They see public policies reflecting the interests not of the consumers of health and welfare services but increasingly of the providers. Some also see a degree of class conflict between the New Class and the old middle class occupied in the production and distribution of material goods and services. Add to this the not entirely separate conflict of interest between bureaucrats and entrepreneurs, between wealth-takers and wealth-producers.

The 'public interest' movement

All this bears on the legitimacy of the public interest pressure group network and its health campaigns. These groups base their legitimacy largely on the claim that they have no vested interests other than the public interest. As such they believe their lobby is socially and morally superior to that of profit-motivated business and industry. Therefore, they claim that they should have a superior say in public policy formulation.

On the same grounds they claim a right to a sort of affirmative action if not automatic credibility from the media as well as government. They depict themselves as citizen Davids fighting corporate Goliaths. They expect to be taken at their word in contrast to untrustworthy commercial special interests which should be taken, if at all, with a grain of salt. If public interest white hats are caught out factually misleading the public, say in a shock-horror, consumer-scare campaign, this should never be attributed to manipulation, but to innocent error, or at the most, to forgivable over-enthusiasm for the public interest.

Preventive health policy and anti-business attitudes

Turning from vested interest to ideology, a significant anti-business element is evident in the so-called public interest movement. If there is one universal theme in worldwide public interest health campaigns which distinguishes them from conventional health care action, it is the almost total emphasis on what they call preventive rather than curative action. The official slogan of the World Health Organisation is now the somewhat utopian 'Health for All by the Year 2000'.

Prevention is a powerfully attractive approach, especially these days when escalating health budgets are becoming nightmares, not only for governments but for taxpayers. And who today would deny that prevention is better than cure? Or that health and safety should not be a high social value - not exclusive but high - for economic as well as social and individual human reasons?

The trouble is that while positively attractive, prevention does open a Pandora's box politically. On the negative side, it creates something of a political gold rush among those who want legitimising reasons for state intervention into both business and society. It also leads to a good deal of unhealthy politicisation of health policy, and medical and scientific bodies.

In Australia, and presumably elsewhere, it is increasingly doctors of economics, sociology, and politics rather than of medicine who are to the fore in determining health policy. Social workers and lawyers are becoming more prominent in community health centres than qualified medical doctors and nurses. Similarly, there is a noticeable tendency in some medical, statistical, and scientific bodies towards what is euphemistically called regulatory science or advocacy science. It might more accurately be called politicised science, ie 'we're not here to study the world, we're here to change it'.

Misuse of prevention policies can amount to declaring open a regulatory hunting season not only on commercial products and advertising, but also on professional services and business management generally. In this context, it is pertinent to note the recent decision by the British Labour Party finally to remove nationalisation of industry from its party platform. But note also that it replaced nationalisation with the policy of strengthening regulatory agencies. In other words, it is simply not necessary for the state to own industries to control them. There are more ways than one to skin a cat. Ownership can be a nuisance, and is now historically discredited. Control is what is important and that is possible by regulation.

This new post-Cold War interventionist approach is not confined to Britain or its Labour Party. As mentioned earlier, the New Class provides a disproportionately influential constituency for any political party or faction that pushes big Government intervention. And what more attractive justification could any politician find than saving voters from avoidable illness and death.

Additionally, anti-capitalist ideologues in affluent countries often find that arguing health exploitation by profit-motivated business taps left-wing traditions and arouses more politically useful moral passion nowadays than does old-fashioned wage-exploitation.

In this respect it is useful to make a few simplified comparisons and contrasts between the rise of the trade union movement internationally and the more recent rise of the so-called public interest movement. One of its leading gurus in the International Organisation of Consumer Unions has expressed the view that the public interest movement will become a more effective vehicle for what he called progressive social change than the trade union movement.

The logic behind that remark is that there has always been an inbuilt moderating element in the mainstream trade union movement. Its leaders were accountable to their constituencies in a way that many public interest group leaders are not. Many public interest leaders are effectively self-appointed, and often based in organisations with miniscule voting memberships, effectively controlled by their officials. Trade union constituencies may want a bigger share of the profits, but they do not want to kill the goose that lays the (mostly) golden eggs of jobs and salaries.

But what skin is it off a tenured bureaucrat's or public interest group leader's nose if businesses go bust because of their legal suits, boycotts, consumer scares, and increased regulation, taxes and costs? They are insulated from the effects of their campaigns in a way trade unionists never have been.

Anti-business attitudes increasingly widespread

The attitude that free enterprise, and probably capitalism in general are bad for your health is not some sort of disembodied social tendency. Increasingly it is based in a burgeoning network of influential national and international activist organisations targeting public policy.

To cite just one example, that of the International Organisation of Consumer Unions (IOCU), the international peak council of national consumerist groups, which claims to represent billions of consumers in 70 countries around the world. It has appreciable influence with UN agencies, particularly the World Health Organisation. It is one of WHO's accredited policy formulating Non-Government Organisations. It also carries weight with the European Community bureaucracy.

Since 1960 the IOCU has been the prime mover in creating several other international activist coalitions. IOCU subsidiaries now include Health Action International (HAI), Consumer Interpol (CI), International Babyfood Action Network (IBFAN), and Pesticides Action Network (PAN). It has also forged links with numerous compatible groups including the United States-based Institute of Policy Studies and Interfaith Centre on Corporate Responsibility.

The IOCU agenda covers much more than such conventional consumer services as product testing, price comparisons, consumer education and publications. It pushes wide-ranging regulatory codes which many consider radical. When the President of the Consumers' Federation of America, Rhoda Karpatkin, became President of the IOCU a few years ago she emphasised what she termed the 'macro socio-economic role' of that organisation. She called on governments to increase food and nutrition programs, low cost housing, health care and legal aid. Irrespective of the merits of such programs, the IOCU's call shows that is has an agenda much wider than and different from what many people would conceive as consumer protection.

Calls for consumerist 'revolution'

The scope of the IOCU's aims was emphasised at its 11th World Congress by Anwar Fazal, its past President and considered by many to be its most dynamic influence. He said; 'Nothing short of a revolution will substantially alter the character of the business system and its ally advertising'. He added that 'that revolution has now begun the world over'. Fazal also stated:

> The 1980s will see a global consumer movement that is the strongest ever in history. With our new way of global organising, and with our new power, multinationals will have to change on a significant level.
>
> We have now got muscle globally to deal with them in a way that we never had before: power to organise globally, to organise boycotts, direct actions, share-holder actions, power to embarrass them for engaging in unconscionable activities. (*Multinational Monitor*, July 1982)

Among the IOCU's critics is the Washington-based conservative think-tank, the Heritage Foundation, which replied that Fazal:

> has spawned a "new wave" of extremist, anti-enterprise consumer organisations...He uses distortions to undermine the multinational corporations and the private sector approach to development. (*Multinational Monitor*, January 1983)

Conclusion

What then is the economic, social and political impact of the briefly sketched model of the modern health phenomenon I have presented?

Firstly, the mushrooming of groups like the IOCU seems to reflect the rise of strong new secular religions whose characteristics include opposition to economic growth, industrial technology and competitive capitalism. To them wealth production is something of a health hazard; for many of us their type of health promotion may prove a wealth hazard.

These secular religions or ideologies seem to attract the New Class and suit their vested interests. Essentially, they are establishmentarians. They want (perhaps demand is a better word) to see the traditional separation of church and state reversed and their values established as official state ideology. Opposition views and lifestyles are seen as sinful. Many have no use for the tolerance that has been a keystone of liberal democratic societies. If my rough model has any value, the economic, social and political consequences should be obvious.

A final point. Some conservative critics balk at this sort of criticism of the public interest movement. They see it as an attack on the very voluntary mediating institutions that thinkers like De Tocqueville saw as vital to protecting civil society against the ever-encroaching power of the modern state. But I believe the opposite is true. So-called public interest organisations and their New Class constituencies are becoming little more than adjuncts of state bureaucracy. They are becoming a force for rather than against centralised state power.

4   The Health Activists: Educators or Propagandists?

Digby Anderson

The real debate: health education versus health activism

Today's Americans are 'ducking' personal, individual responsibility while 'telling everyone else what to do'. They are 'decadent Puritans' refusing to accept responsibility for ill-health and other misfortunes, 'banishing the concept of bad luck' and blaming their troubles instead on the companies which provided them with services or goods, the beer, the ice-cream or the cigar. Along with the passing of the buck goes a killjoy intolerance of 'the fellow who prefers cream and an early coronary to self-absorption in a costly gym building muscles he will never need'.

The denunciation is not mine but comes from a leader in *The Economist*.[1] It has not got it quite right, in my view, and we have certainly got our decadent Puritans in the UK as well, but what it does do is pinpoint the divergence between those who see modern health and lifestyle matters as the individual consumer's responsibility and those who wish to control and regulate supply. The activists who implore more regulations essentially want political or legal controls. Those who emphasise individual consumer and parental responsibility also want controls, but self-control and informal social control. Many would see one way to self and social control as through better education, and informed choices. The dispute then is not between those who want legal and governmental controls and those who would do nothing but between health educationists and those who would politicise health.

My background, prior to my current post, is in health education research where I produced one of the first UK textbooks on the subject. I take the educators' side in the dispute. By health education I mean specifically: families, intermediate community

39

agencies and schools giving children at school information about behaviour-related illness, encouraging them to think about the values involved in approving or rejecting certain behaviour and developing their capacity to take decisions and the responsibility for them. In the health care field, it means helping doctors and others to communicate effectively with their patients in the treatment of actual illnesses and in warning of conditions at risk. But most important of all, health education also occurs spontaneously when there is free public debate about health and behaviour.

What must be stressed is that health education with its emphasis on helping the individual make responsible decisions is fundamentally opposed to the new politicised health-activism or health-promotion which involves activists and governments taking mass level decisions for different individuals and imposing mass solutions - regulations, propaganda and other interventions on them.

In May 1991 a Government document was leaked which discussed setting targets for a 30 per cent reduction in coronary heart disease by the year 2000.[2] This is to be achieved by reducing the proportion of the population eating high levels of fats from 85 per cent to 50 per cent. Another target is to reduce the numbers smoking. But what if the millions who make up this 35 per cent, aware of any dangers in smoking or eating fat rate them dangers worth taking? Are they to be coerced? How likely is it that their myriad individual decisions should miraculously add up to some government target? Either the target is a pious and empty hope or it is indeed coercive. The document is revealingly titled *The Health of the Nation*, as if health and happiness were a state of mass well-being to be decided by government. Nothing could be further from the educational goal of individuals making decisions and taking responsibility for them.

An example of divergence: the case of alcohol

Health education is not about outcomes but processes, not about predictions or intentions to change the health state of nations but empowering individuals to take considered decisions. Consider how the two diverge. The health educationist would like to see adults and especially children aware that drinking to excess can ruin livers, livelihoods and families; that drinking when driving kills innocent others; that drunkenness is associated with crime and abuse and alcohol abuse results in work absenteeism and other so-called social costs. But the educationist also wants the adult or child to be aware that of the 90 per cent of Britons who regularly drink, 90 per cent of men and 96 per cent of women do so within the stringent limits currently fashionable; that small amounts of alcohol seem beneficial to health and that drinking is enjoyable; that most road deaths caused by drink are caused by those well above the legal limit; and that economists cannot agree on the social costs of alcohol. In short, that for the vast majority of the population, moderate drinking under self and social controls is pleasant and beneficial not something continually to worry about. Compare this with the activist approach.

Health activists ignore the pleasures and the enormous success rate of the many with their drinking. They are set on making a mass problem out of a minority one. Their level of 'dangerous drinking' was reduced from five to one or two large drinks a day within a space of two years or so, a reduction not accompanied by any mass of new evidence. At this rate, it will soon be zero. Within the same period those who had suggested one drink-free day a week, started calling for two or three.[3]

Claims of health activists increasingly extreme

Notice first the tendency of the health claims to become more and more extreme. Now the food-faddist and neo-prohibitionist and anti-smoking bandwagons are rolling, they are not going to be stop-ped by any modest change in habits - there is a new scare every few months. The tendency to extremism is, of course, fuelled by the need to make claims more worrying than last year's in order to get media attention. Then, notice that the more widely the problem is defined, the more it appears to justify mass political solutions. If the problem is not just two to five per cent of drinkers, not just the severely obese or those eating extremely unbalanced diets, but potentially the whole population, the whole 'nation', then what better than a government policy, a Ministry for Food as is being proposed in Britain, a new law, or this or that Europe-wide legisla-tion, such as the EEC Commission is proposing.

Thus the activists' solutions: intervention in the livestock market to subsidise leaner animals, differential taxes on products they decree 'unhealthy', advertising bans on such products, their messages standardised as the sole state-approved descriptions of products on labels - mass and extreme solutions.

The constant push to inflate the problem to mass levels inevitably means bunching together individuals who have one problem with those who have a different problem and the many who have none at all. Thus claims that there is something wrong with the nation's diet suggest that there is a diet suitable for all, that nursing mothers, children, bed-ridden elderly people, active and sedentary men should subscribe to some common regime. A nutritionist at one of the London hospitals has expressed concern that this may lead to dangerous neglect of the special needs of sub-groups and cites 'reports of children with growth failure as a con-sequence of high-fibre diets (so bulky that insufficient energy is eaten) ...iron deficiency, anaemia in older women almost certainly exacerbated by low-fat diets which also happen to be low in iron'.

Mass 'solutions' ignore individual needs

Equally grave, the energy and funds devoted to blasting broad range food propaganda at the whole nation, most of whom have no problem, leaves fewer resources for identifying the few who are genuinely at risk and treating them. And to make the message fit the mass, it has to be massaged. It must be simple. Contradictions and variations in the evidence must be suppressed. That London nutritionist was joined by several others in a book my institute published called *A Diet of Reason*.[4] For instance, on salt the expert lists some of the complications:

> The effect of salt restriction upon blood pressure levels is more controversial. Some studies have shown a small but significant fall in blood pressure: others have not...Salt restriction seems to have little effect on the milder de-grees of high blood pressure...Salt restriction may there-fore by helpful in some cases to a minor degree although it alone is usually insufficient to bring pressure down to normal. For the remaining patients and for the rest of the population it seems to have little effect. Even when blood pressure is lowered this tells us nothing about why it is

raised in the first place. Bleeding is an equally effective method of lowering blood pressure yet no-one claims that an excess of blood is responsible...The salt "sensitivity" of some hypertensive patients...appears to be a consequence and not a cause of high blood pressure.[5]

There are similar complications on fibre and, for instance on obesity. Dr Passmore having noted three levels of obesity points out that 'obesity is a serious disorder' but most of those so classified are properly described as plump. 'Plump people do not need to reduce their weight for health reasons, though they should watch their weight and see that they do not become obese'.[6]

The mass solutions advocated by the activists have little regard for the diversity of consumers. Rather as socialists speak of 'the working class' as having a common interest and claim to represent it, so many health and consumer activists imply that consumers are a class which has an interest which they represent. But consumers have different health needs, different pleasures in eating and drinking. Their preferences not only diverge but compete. A mass solution is bound to be a coercive one for many and a crude one for all. In the UK, health activists cannot be assumed to represent the consumer. Some do indeed represent particular group interests, eg doctors. Others represent no-one except themselves, yet others represent a section of consumers. Yet many sell their ideas as if on the consumers' behalf. Nowhere is this more so than in the debate about labelling.

Compulsory food labelling: information or propaganda?

The consumer, they say, has a right to know what he or she is buying. But what if the information one consumer wants to know is not the same as another. And is 'information' what the activists demand? Some consumers might want the ingredients given according to scientific convention. Most would neither want nor understand them. What the activists want is not information but directions and warnings. Some of these are not information but opinions. Others depend for their use on who the consumer is. In fields where there is scientific disagreement, they are simply propaganda. They are usually that anyway since space rarely permits the necessary qualifications truthful information would demand. And label regulation is largely unnecessary. Sellers are now aware that there is a market in messages. Those who supply the information most customers want sell more.

Many of the messages proposed for standardised labelling are nothing to do with consumers. They simply represent the obsessions of the activists. There is now a vast line of activists pushing to get their hobbyhorses included on the tiny label on a packet or bottle of food, drink or medicine. If they had their way we would all have to be told all the ingredients, which were dangerous, at what level of dosage even if it were 1,000 times the normal amount consumed, and for whom; if the danger or safety had been established by animal experimentation, under what conditions the animals had been kept, the arrangements made for the retirement conditions of the animals when their experimental life was over. There would be instructions on storage and usage, standard instructions and therefore necessarily in terms and at length suitable for the stupidest and most incompetent user; which ingredients were natural and which not with a five line definition of 'natural'; what environmental effect, if any, the production of the container, label and product had had or of any their consumption might have. The price would have to be expressed relative to weight, size, concentration and 20 other measures to enable comparison with other products. Large declarations would have to be made as to whether any company involved in the production of the packaging, contents or label, any supplying industry or any bank providing them with funds had, at any time had or known anyone who had connections with South Africa or whatever the current Boo country is; whether the pay and conditions of the workforces producing the container, label and product satisfied whatever standards the activists pluck out of the sky as suitable; and the contribution of the product and its consumption to ethnic harmony. One might as well attach to the tiny packet an encyclopaedia, plus a dozen political billboards and be done with it.

Competing sources of information educative and a fundamental part of any democracy

Education is a far simpler way and the kind of education is the third I mentioned, which does not even have to be set up. It occurs naturally in a democracy characterised by public debate and competing claims. Quite simply when people want information and opinions and are prepared to pay for them, they will be supplied. And not mass and standardised: each person will get the information he needs. This is the nub of the dispute, dear to the activists about advertising bans.

Currently there is no lack of information and opinions on the relation between behaviour and health. The universities and professions produce their journals, the bookshops and magazine stalls are full of publications, the producers advertise and the activists put out their opinions in reports. The same process occurs in the electronic media. This is public debate, information from diverse sources competing for consumers with diverse information appetites. It is, in its way, an educational process. And it is far less dangerous than any one source monopolising information and deciding that there should be one message.

But the standardisation of labelling and the restriction of advertising are just that, moves toward single source information backed by governmental decree as the official source. Advertising is not always truthful. It can manipulate dreams, fears and illusions. But then so can politicians. There is no sin known to commercial speech which politicians have not used and excelled in. Any argument for restricting freedom of commercial speech is potentially an argument for restricting freedom of political speech with all that entails.

Moreover, it is currently advertising revenue which sustains the diversity of publications which carry the political views and the features on health and behaviour. Both directly and indirectly, the freedom of a free society is bound up with the freedom of commercial speech and multi-source information.

No place for health activism in a free society

Health promotion or activism has a weak knowledge base, as other contributors to this book show, and I have pointed out that it is also indiscriminate, unable to take account of people's different needs and wants. Its bias to mass, standardised solutions also means it has to simplify and distort the truth about the complicated links between health and behaviour. It places a low value on freedom, responsibility and self-determination. Because of these characteristics the health activists in Britain are sometimes called paternalists, sometimes nannies, or consumer-socialists, or in the case of those who want to engineer people's diets for them in vast five-year plans, food-Leninists. But I am more concerned with what they are not. For though they may hide behind the term health education, what the health activists are not is educationists. Indeed their mass, top-down and extremist solutions are the very opposite of what is usually called education in a free society.

Notes and references

1. *The Economist*, 14 May, 1991
2. As leaked to and discussed in the British press during May 1991 and subsequently contained in the Government Green Paper published in June 1991.
3. For a further discussion of the issues raised here, see D Anderson (ed), *Drinking to Your Health: the allegations and the evidence*, London: Social Affairs Unit, 1989.
4. D Anderson (ed), *A Diet of Reason: sense and nonsense in the healthy eating debate*, London: Social Affairs Unit, 1986.
5. J D Swales, 'Salt and high blood pressure: a study in education, persuasion and naïveté in *Diet of Reason*, ibid., p.60.
6. Reg Passmore, 'Obesity and the plumpness which needs no diet', in *Diet of Reason*, op.cit., p.100.

5   Risk-Factor Epidemiology: Science or Non-science?

Petr Skrabanek

The changing role of epidemiology

Until about 1950, epidemiologists studied patterns of infectious diseases, particularly the more common ones. The term *epidemia* was used since the time of Hippocrates for widespread diseases affecting whole populations (*epidemeo*, to be among a people). As infectious diseases gradually became less prevalent, in part due to the discovery of antibiotics, epidemiologists had to turn their attention to something else. It is no longer clear what is the raison d'être of epidemiology, as judged for example from 23 different definitions of epidemiology, collected by Lilienfeld.[1] He points out that 'the idea that epidemiology is the study of anything is a very modern innovation'. In a sense, there is an epidemic of epidemiologists who are short of diseases suitable for their investigations.

The main preoccupation of epidemiologists is now the association game. This consists in searching for associations between 'diseases of civilisation' and 'risk factors'. The 'diseases of civilisation' are heart disease and cancer. The curse of civilisation is that people are deprived of dying young of simple infectious diseases, such as tuberculosis, smallpox, or the plague. The 'risk factors' studied by epidemiologists are either personal characteristics (age, sex, race, weight, height, diet, habits, customs, vices) or situational characteristics (geography, occupation, environment, air, water, sun, gross national product, stress, density of doctors).

Important associations, such as liver cirrhosis or Korsakoff's psychosis in alcoholism, retinopathy or foot gangrene in diabetes, aortic lesions or sabre tibias in syphilis, lung cancer in uranium ore miners, bladder cancer in workers with aniline dyes, are not discovered by epidemiologists but by clinicians, and they are not called 'associations' but the manifestations, signs, or complications of diseases which are their causes.

'Discoveries' of epidemiologists are of a more general nature. For example, to quote from the announcement of a conference on the prevention of cancer, which was organised by the Cancer Education Co-ordinating Group of the United Kingdom and Republic of Ireland, in association with the Health Education Authority, and held at the Royal Society of Medicine in London on November 21, 1989,

> A report commissioned by the European Commission found that one-third of all cancer deaths are attributable to cigarette smoking, one third could be attributable to diet including the consumption of alcohol, and another third are because of other factors including sexual and re-productive behaviour and occupational activities. The Committee of European Cancer Experts who produced the report recommend a 10 Point Code to help avoid the risk of developing cancers. The adoption of this Code by the public is the main aim of the "Europe Against Cancer" initiative.

Though there is some verbal hedging ('attributable' instead of 'caused'; 'could be' instead of 'is'), the message comes across loud and clear that the causes of cancer are well known and it is now up to the public to stop whingeing and start behaving. The message can be simplified, so that it is more easily remembered, as: 'smok-ing, drinking and sex are three main causes of cancer'. Other reputable epidemiologists are on record as saying that up to 70 per cent of all cancers are caused by diet. There is a certain plausibility in such claims, as it has been shown that there is a strong association between eating any of the three major constituents of the human diet (protein, fat, carbohydrate) and subsequent deaths, many of them from cancer.

The association game has three possible outcomes: positive association, negative association, or no association. As any of these three outcomes are generally deemed to be 'interesting', 'controversial', or 'in need of further research', they all get published. 'No association' is an uncommon outcome, since in most studies at least 'a tendency towards' a positive or negative association can be shown. Considering how many cancers exist, and how many items of diet can be entered into the game, the number of possible combinations is staggering and opens new vistas for the generations of epidemiologists to come. The scope of epidemiological research has been widened enormously by including 'passive' exposures to invisible electromagnetic waves, whether from home appliances, overhead wires, nuclear power stations or space, passive exposures to other people's smoke or to air pollutants (we inhale 20,000 litres of air a day!).

Associations nothing new, often random and seldom simple

As an example I shall use cabbage consumption, believed to be negatively associated with cancer, and coffee consumption, believed to be positively associated with heart disease. It is always tacitly understood, though rarely explicitly stated that 'association' implies in some way causation, since without such an understanding there would be no point in reporting a chance association. I am using cabbage as an example simply because I have just received the latest issue of *Progress Against Cancer* published by the Canadian Cancer Society, and on the last page there was the reproduction of a poster, issued by the Canadian Cancer Society, with the following text:

> Cancer Prevention. You can have a hand in it. The Canadian Cancer Society recommends that you include more vegetables from the cabbage family in your diet. These include brussel sprouts, broccoli and cauliflower. These vegetables may protect you against the risk of cancer.

This educational message is based on epidemiological research, but Cato the Elder (234-149 BC) wrote in his treatise *On Agriculture* that 'cabbage surpasses all other vegatables...an ulcer of the breast and a cancer can be healed by the application of macerated cabbage'. Similarly, Dioscorides in *De materia medica* recommended direct application of cabbage on tumours to cause them to shrink. Apparently there is something in cabbage which has been exciting human minds for the past 2000 years.

There are snags, however. B N Ames and L S Gold found that

cabbage is as strong a promoter of carcinogenesis as dioxin and that 'a 100-gram helping of broccoli might present roughly 20 times the possible hazard of the dioxin reference dose'.[3] To complicate matters even more, Marshall et al reported in their study of risk factors for cervical cancer that

> most notably, cruciferous vegetables [cabbage, coleslaw, turnips, but *not* broccoli] were associated with an *increased* [their emphasis] cervical cancer risk. The significance of the noted risk enhancement is greater than that of the protective effect of vitamin A. An earlier study indicated that cruciferous vegetable ingestion is protective against colon cancer. As noted then, there is abundant biochemical evidence that cruciferae could be protective in the gut, so that induction of aryl hydroxylase activity could be protective in the gut and carcinogenic in the lung and cervix.[4]

While there is no good reason to believe that cabbage has anything to do with cancer, it is characteristic of epidemiological literature that such chance associations as between cabbage in diet and mortality from some cancer are discussed in terms 'protective' or 'carcinogenic'.

Coffee drinking was always suspect as a 'risk factor'. King Charles issued a proclamation for the suppression of coffee houses in 1675, in which he

> commanded all manner of persons, that they or any of them do not presume from and after the tenth day of January next ensuing, to keep any public coffee house, or to utter or sell by retail, in his, her or their house or houses (to be spent or consumed within the same) any coffee, chocolet, sherbett or tea, as they will answer the contrary at their utmost peril.

In 1695, the Medical School of Paris announced that coffee deprived men of their generative powers. Coffee drinkers, just like the victims of self-abuse, became shrivelled shadows of their former selves, with haggard looks and an uncontrollable tremor.

More recently, in 1988, a group of epidemiologists from the National Institute of Environmental Health Sciences at Research Triangle Park, North Carolina, reported in *The Lancet* that 'women who consumed more than the equivalent of one cup of coffee per day were half as likely to become pregnant as women who drank less'.[5] On the other hand, according to a news item in the *Daily Telegraph* of January 19, 1990, a study carried out among 744 people in Michigan, showed that those who drank coffee were full of beans, that is, they were more sexually active than those who did not drink coffee.

A group of epidemiologists from the Department of Health Services in Berkeley studied an association between coffee drinking and spontaneous abortions: results were inconclusive but suggestive of an association, particularly in women who suffered from the nausea of pregnancy. The authors concluded that 'further study is warranted'.[7]

Scores of epidemiological studies have been devoted to analysing associations between coffee and bladder cancer, colorectal cancer, ovarian cancer, pancreatic cancer, kidney cancer, breast cancer, hypertension, hip fracture, premenstrual syndrome, and childhood diabetes. The list is not exhaustive. Bruce Ames reported that 'of 247 volatile natural chemicals reported in coffee (mostly pyrolysis products) 10 have been tested in chronic animal cancer tests and 7 are carcinogenic (eg furfural, catechol). The total amount of rodent carcinogens are roughly 9 mg/cup.[8] However, the majority of studies on coffee and health have dealt with the risk of coronary heart disease in coffee drinkers. In a recent editorial in the *British Medical Journal* the editorialist reviewed 24 such studies.[9]

The plot has thickened since the most recent studies have exculpated caffeine and incriminated decaffeinated coffee instead. One of the chemicals used in the process of decaffeinisation is methylene chloride. This was shown to have a carcinogenic effect in rats who were administered methylene chloride at a dose of 1,000 mg/kg/day (equivalent of 24 million cups of decaffeinated coffee per day).[10] This does not quite explain the effect of coffee on heart disease, but, as the editorialist concluded 'before we can decide whether decaffeinated coffee increases the risk of heart disease longer studies with multiple assessment of exposure to decaffeinated and caffeinated coffee are needed'.

The new epidemiology provides justification for infinite research - and funding

The advantage of this approach is that one never gets a clear answer, which allows for studying the problem indefinitely. Alvin Weinberg, in discussing the probability of extremely improbable events (such as our examples of coffee causing various diseases, or cabbage causing or preventing cancer) introduced the concept of trans-science, by which he means problems which hang on the answers to questions which can be asked of science and yet which cannot be answered by science.[11]

In one of his examples, which is relevant for current epidemiological investigations into the effects of low-level radiation on health, the trans-scientific question was whether a 150-millirem dose of X-radiation would increase the spontaneous mutation rate in mice by 0.5 percent, as calculated by linear extrapolation from higher doses. To answer this question by a direct experiment would require 8 billion mice. And even if such an experiment could have been carried out, the relevance for humans would be unclear and the experiment would have to be repeated on eight billion men, to be sure!

As so many scares have been disseminated by epidemiological research into risk factors, further research is often called for to confirm or to deny the rumours. Recently, a group of American epidemiologists provided reassurance to vasectomised men that they are *not* at an increased risk of dying from heart disease. This will hold until other researchers will confirm the initial positive association.

When too many such conflicting observations have accumulated, a call is made for meta-analysis and possibly a consensus conference. As meta-analysis is increasingly used at consensus conferences, and invited meta-analysts conjure metaphysical 'statistical significance' from the insignificant, like the alchemists of old converting dross into false gold, the time will soon come for the metaconsensus of consensus.[12] In fact, earlier this year, the King Edward's Hospital Fund convened a meeting on consensus, and at one point they 'all agreed'.[13]

Risk factors largely irrelevant to search for causal mechanisms

The last official count of the risk factors for coronary heart disease was 246.[14] Since then many others have been discovered by assiduous epidemiologists. Some of them are listed in and compared with a selected list of risk factors for scurvy compiled before the cause of scurvy was known, that is the lack of vitamin C.[15] The plethora of risk factors leads some epidemiologists to postulate the so-called multifactorial aetiology. While in a certain sense, all

Table 1: Risk factors for coronary heart disease and scurvy

Risk factors for coronary heart disease

age	divorced parents
male sex	illegitimate birth
mother tongue English	no church attendance
urban residence	Jewish religion
altitude	not being a Mormon
cold weather	alcoholism
noise	total abstinence
extramarital sex	obesity
snoring	slow beard growth
baldness	homocystinaemia
short stature	high blood sugar
not eating mackerel	low plasma zinc
no varsity athletics	no garlic
type A personality	high white cell count
work > 60 hrs/week	vasectomy
good financial status	early menopause
low socioeconomic status	contraceptive pill
1-child family	coffee
being > 4th child	passive smoking
low education	too much milk
intelligent wife	too little milk
unloving wife	chlorinated water
non-supportive boss	widowhood

Risk factors for scurvy

bad butter	tobacco
bad diet	unleavened bread
copper boilers	cold
debauchery	dampness
dejection	external causes
distilled spirits	inactivity
fruit lack	low marsh ground
gluttony	sea air
infection	season change
mercury	constitution
spoiled floor	heredity
sugar	melancholy disposition

events are multifactorial, even such trivial occurrences as being hit on the head with a chunk of frozen urine discarded from an overflying aircraft (the factors include, the speed of the aircraft, the speed and the direction of the wind, the time spent at a crossword during breakfast, the reason and the speed of the fatal walk, and myriads of others), we do not use the term 'multifactorial' when the cause of an event is understood.

Risk factors have nothing to do with causes. They are risk *markers*, but they are neither sufficient nor necessary to explain the risk. Thus, for example, the possession of a driving licence is a risk marker for death in a car accident, marshes are a risk marker for malaria, and homosexuality a risk marker for AIDS. The knowledge of risk factors rarely, if ever, contributes to the elucidation of causal mechanisms. At best, it may provide a hint as to where to look for the cause. When the cause of tuberculosis was still unknown, numerous risk factors were described, none of which was of any use to Koch in his laboratory studies leading to the discovery of the necessary cause - the mycobacterium.

It is the intimation by epidemiologists that they hold the key to the causes of diseases and their prevention which makes them overstep their brief and join the moralists in their preaching how to avoid death by being good, clean-living citizens.

The hope that by searching for risk factors, the causal mechanisms will somehow come to light is misplaced. Such an approach is the rich source of false leads. Thus, when the first cases of AIDS appeared in the USA, risk-factor epidemiologists looked at ethnic and religious background, alcohol and tobacco use, diet, residential and occupational histories, sexual practices and drug use. They concluded that the use of amyl nitrate ('poppers') was the strongest risk factor, implying a causal link.[16] The strength of association was of the same order as for smoking and lung cancer, yet this lead was a red herring.

Or, to use another example, when oestrogen-replacement therapy was thought to be a risk factor for coronary heart disease, two 'definitive' studies were published in the same issue of the prestigious *New England Journal of Medicine*: one showed a significant negative association, and the other, a significant positive association, implying causative or protective mechanisms. It would be reasonable to conclude that at least one of these epidemiological studies was wrong, and possibly both. The accompanying editorial was painful reading.[17] The editorialist admitted that both studies 'appear[ed] to be methodologically sound'. The most likely explanation for the disagreement between the two studies was that such studies

> and by implication the results of countless other observational studies, are subject to a great deal more variability than is captured by the usual kinds of statistical tests and confidence limits. I simply cannot tell from present evidence whether these hormones add to the risk of various cardiovascular diseases, diminish the risk, or leave it unchanged, and must resort to the investigator's great cop-out: more research is needed.[18]

This kind of 'science' is not exactly Nobel prize stuff.

In conclusion

Alvan Feinstein, casting a cool eye at some of the nonsense going on in the name of risk-factor epidemiology, suggested that

> until the new paradigms, methods, and data are developed, non-epidemiological scientists and members of the lay public will have to use common sense and their own scientific concepts to evaluate the reported evidence.[19]

Notes and References

1. D E Lilienfeld, 'Definitions of epidemiology', *American Journal of Epidemiology*, 107, 1978, pp.87-90.
2. Canadian Cancer Society, *Progress Against Cancer*, Vol.44, No.1, 1991.
3. B N Ames and L S Gold, 'Misconceptions regarding environmental pollution and cancer causation' in M Moore (ed), *Health Risks and the Media: Perspectives on Media Coverage of Risk Assessment and Health*, Chicago: American Medical Association, 1989, pp.19-34.
4. J R Marshall, S Graham, T Byers, M Swanson, J Brasure, 'Diet and smoking in the epidemiology of cancer of the cervix', *Journal of the National Cancer Institute*, 70, 1983, pp.847-851.
5. *The Lancet*, 24 December, 1988, p.1453.
6. *The Daily Telegraph*, 19 January, 1990.
7. *American Journal of Epidemiology*, 132, 1990, p.796.
8. B N Ames, 'Endogenous vs. exogenous factors as major cancer risk determinants', *Proceedings of the American Association for Cancer Research*, 31, 1990, pp.512-513.
9. *British Medical Journal*, 6 April, 1991, p.804.

10. D H Morris, 'Decaffeination of coffee', *Journal of the American Medical Association*, 254, 1985, p.825.
11. A M Weinberg, 'Science and trans-science', *Minerva*, 10, 1972, pp.207-222.
12. P Skrabanek, 'Nonsensus consensus', *The Lancet*, 335, 1990, pp.1446-1447.
13. *British Medical Journal*, 6 April 1991, p.800.
14. P N Hopkins and R R Williams, 'A survey of 246 suggested coronary risk factors, *Atherosclerosis*, 40, 1981, pp.1-52.
15. L M Klevay, 'The role of copper, zinc and other chemical elements in ischemic heart disease', in O M Rennert and W Y Chan (eds), *Metabolism of Metals in Man*, New York : CRC Press, 1984, p.129.
16. J P Vandenbroucke, V P A M Pardoel, 'An autopsy of epidemiological methods: the case of "poppers" in the early epidemic of the acquired immunodeficiency syndrome (AIDS)', *American Journal of Epidemiology*, 129, 1989, pp.455-457.
17. J C Bailar, 'When research results are in conflict', *New England Journal of Medicine*, 313, 1985, pp.1080-1081.
18. A R Feinstein, 'Scientific standards in epidemiological studies of the menace of daily life', *Science*, 242, 1988, pp.1257-1263

6 Scientific Fact or Scientific Self-Delusion: Passive Smoking, Exercise and the New Puritanism

J R Johnstone *

Passive smoking and cancer: the question stated

'Passive smoking' is the inhalation of tobacco smoke produced by other people. Because smoking itself is widely regarded as a cause of ill-health and in particular lung cancer, concern has been expressed that passive smoking might also be harmful. Although both smokers and non-smokers may be passive smokers, most concern has naturally been felt for the non-smoker and that is the question considered here: specifically, does passive smoking cause lung cancer in non-smokers?[1]

The answer necessarily must come from epidemiology, the study of the frequency, distribution and cause of illness and death. It is quite insufficient to quote the evidence that cigarette smoke contains poisons - it certainly does. The Surgeon General's report marshalls a battery of such evidence, but as such it is circumstantial and incomplete. Rhubarb and spinach contain about one percent oxalic acid but we need not quail on being offered Eggs Florentine or Rhubarb and Apple Crumble, even though a lethal dose of oxalic acid is only 10 grams.[2] A properly controlled study would be needed to determine the incidence of rhubarb and spinach poisoning in the community. So too with passive smoking and lung cancer. If the purpose is to frame public policies which may limit individual freedoms, then it is of particular importance that a correct and reliable answer be obtained.

* This chapter is a modified and edited extract from J R Johnstone and C Ulyatt, *Health Scare: The Misuse of Science in Public Health Policy*. Critical Issues No. 14, Perth: Australian Institute For Policy Study, 1991. It appears by permission.

Two kinds of study: case-control and prospective

There are two important kinds of study. In a case-control study, people with lung cancer are examined and compared to similar individuals without lung cancer. How do the individuals in the two groups differ? For example, if 100 non-smokers with lung cancer had all been exposed to tobacco smoke while 100 disease-free neighbours matched for age, sex, race etc, had never been so exposed then this would constitute a strong link between passive smoking and lung cancer. In practice no one expects such clear cut results. If 60 of the lung cancer cases had been exposed compared with 40 of the healthy group then the result would be less clear. The methods of statistics are used to determine whether such a result is 'significant'. Here 'significant' means 'statistically significant'. It has nothing to do with the magnitude of the effect observed. A study which showed that passive smokers were one per cent more likely to contract lung cancer than non-exposed individuals might still have found a significant effect.

The second kind of study is a prospective study. For example, select a group of healthy people married to non-smokers and follow them for 10 or 20 years. Compare them with a similar group of people married to smokers. Which group has the highest incidence of lung cancer and, once again, is the difference significant? A major difficulty with such studies is the time and money required to obtain a result. According to the orthodox view, it takes on average 40 to 50 years of cigarette smoking to induce lung cancer.[3] Only a small proportion will succumb much sooner. Therefore a large population must be studied over a long period if any significant effect is to be detected.

Table 1 summarises the results of prospective studies in men and women, with the duration of the trial and the number of subjects who were followed.

Tables 2 and *3* summarise the results of case control studies in men and women respectively. *Table 4* summarises the results of case control studies of men and women together. The authors of each study are listed first, then the number of (non-smoking) lung cancer cases. In Tables *2, 3* and *4* the source of the cigarette smoke - spouse, other family member, workmates etc, is then given. Different authors have classified the source of the cigarette smoke

Table 1: Lung cancer and passive smoking caused by spouse: prospective studies

Study	Duration (Years)	Men	No.	Women	No.
Garfinkel (1981)	12	·	94,000	○	375,000
Gillis et al (1984)	6	○	827	○	1,917
Hirayama (1981, 1984)	17	↑	20,289	↑	91,540

Notes:
○ = a non-significant result
· = this condition was not examined in the paper
↑ = a positive association

according to their own criteria; I have used the classification which here seems most accurate. The source of the cigarette smoke for the prospective studies was always effectively a spouse.

Table 2: Lung cancer in men and passive smoking: case control studies

Study	No. of cases	Spouse	Children Family	Parents F	M	Work	Leisure	Travel
Akiba et al (1986)	19	○	·	·	·	·	·	·
Buffler et al (1984)	5	·	○	·	·	·	·	·
Correa et al (1983)	8	○	·	○	○	·	·	·
Dalager et al (1986)	29	○	·	○		·	·	·
Kabat and Wynder (1984)	37	○	○	·	·	↑	·	·
Lee et al (1986)	32	○	○	·	·	○	○	○

Notes: As for Table 1

For each category an upward arrow ↑ indicates a positive association ie a passive smoker was significantly more likely to contract lung cancer than someone who was not a passive smoker. (○) indicates no significant association was found and a decimal point (·) indicates that the condition was not examined in the particular study.

59

Table 3: Lung cancer in women and passive smoking: case control studies

Study	No. of cases	Spouse	Children Family	Parents F	M	Work	Leisure	Travel
Akiba et al (1986)	94	o	.	.	.	.	.	.
Buffler et al (1984)	33	.	o	.	.	.	.	.
Chan and Fung (1982)	84	o	.	.	.	.	.	.
Correa et al (1983)	22	↑	.	o	o	.	.	.
Dalager et al (1986)	70	o	.	o		.	.	.
Garfinkel et al (1985)	134	o	.	.	.	.	.	.
Humble et al (1987)	20	o	.	.	.	.	.	.
Kabat and Wynder (1984)	97	o	o	.	.	o	.	.
Koo et al (1984, 1985, 1987)	88	o	o	o		.	.	.
Lee et al (1986)	12	o	o	.	.	o	o	o
Pershagen et al (1987)	77	o	.	.	.	.	.	.
Trichopolous et al (1981, 1983)	77	↑	.	.	.	.	.	.
Wu et al (1985)	31	o	.	o	o	o	.	.

Notes: As for Table 1

The arrows reflect the risk associated with passive smoking, the risk-ratio. In these studies the risk-ratio ranged from approximately three times more likely for the largest positive association to three times less likely for the largest negative association.

Table 4: Lung cancer in men and women and passive smoking: case control studies

Study	No. of cases	Spouse	Children Family	—Parents— F	M	Work	Leisure	Travel
Humble et al (1987)	28	↑	.	.	.	.	.	.
Sandler et al (1985)	2	.	○	○	○	.	.	.

Notes: As for Table 1

Overall the tables summarise the results of 26 studies of lung cancer in non-smoking men, women, and men and women. Of these, 20 revealed no association. Of 51 separate exposure situations (spouse, leisure, etc), 45 revealed no association. The failure to find a positive association in most examples suggests a tenuous connection at most, unless the minority studies are of convincing persuasiveness.

Hirayama studies: wrong turnings in a statistical maze

The most widely quoted results are perhaps those of Hirayama. Hirayama analysed his data with a test devised by N Mantel.[4] Mantel[5] replied in a letter to the *British Medical Journal* in which he expressed concern about ambiguities and omissions in Hirayama's paper. In particular it appeared that in Mantel's test Hirayama had mistaken x for x^2. Mantel provided an arithmetically detailed criticism including Mantel's own calculated values. He concluded 'The question then is whether he has conducted a more refined analysis, about which he is giving us no clues, or he has mistakenly interpreted his x^2 value as a x value'. In other words, had Hirayama simply blundered, as even the best of us can do? Hirayama replied to Mantel with the sentence: 'The validity of the significance test used in my paper was kindly confirmed by prominent statisticians in many institutes, including the US National Cancer Institute and the Massachusetts Institute of Technology'.[6] With an appeal to unnamed authorities Hirayama therefore dismissed Mantel's queries without answering. In any other area of science - or indeed intellectual discourse generally - this would be enough to negate Hirayama's contribution.

However he went further and added new information in the form of a histogram *(Fig. 1)*, which revealed some extraordinary results. Rutsch showed that from Hirayama's data it could be deduced that lung cancer was commoner for non-smoking unmarried women than for the non-smoking wives of smokers.[7] Hirayama agreed with Rutsch but noted that most of the 'unmarried' women were widows, adding 'Although their late or former husbands' smoking habits were not asked about at the time of enrolment there is little doubt that the majority of them were smokers'.[8] Inadequate data collection, it appears, leaves little room for doubt.

Figure 1

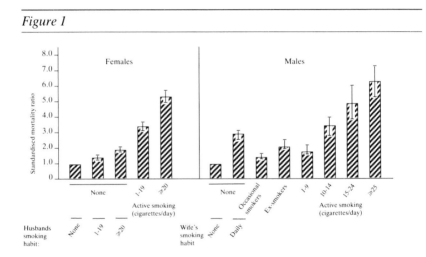

Other strange features were described. Non-smoking men with smoking wives were as likely to get lung cancer as occasional smokers, if not more so. Lee pointed out that in effect this meant that a cigarette apparently had the same carcinogenic effects on a person whether it was smoked by him or by someone else![9] Because 'active' smokers must necessarily breathe the same air as 'passive' smokers this would be a remarkable result indeed.[10] Surely 'active' smokers should get a double dose – smoke they inhale while their cigarette is in their mouth, plus the polluted air they breathe between puffs. Lee went further and showed that Hirayama's 11 printed confidence intervals[11] were all in error by factors of up to 1000 per cent.

Figure 2

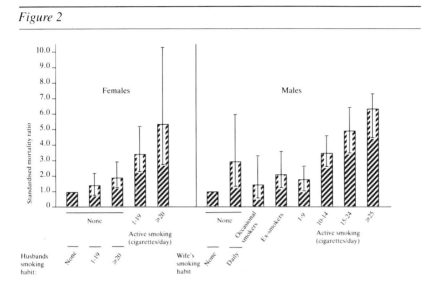

In reply to this new criticism Hirayama[12] admitted that his evidence appeared to show that it mattered not whether a cigarette was actively or passively smoked. His response to the errors pointed out by Lee was 'I regret that errors have been found in the 95 per cent confidence intervals shown in the Figure in my last letter. The correct values are given in the accompanying Figure *(Figure 2)*. The errors do not, however, influence the substance of my letter'. This history must encourage reservations about both his 1981 work and his later paper.[13]

The Trichopolous studies: more confusion

Trichopolous originally presented the results of his study for 40 non-smoking women with lung cancer.[14] He compared them with 149 controls who did not have lung cancer. The results as risk-ratios[15] for women whose husbands were non-smokers, ex-smokers, 1-20 cigarettes/day and 21+/day are shown in *Table 5*.

Burch[16] drew attention to a puzzling feature of the original

Table 5: Risk-ratios for lung cancer in non-smoking women: data of Trichopolous et al (1981, 1983)

	Smoking habit of husband			
	Non-smoker	Ex-smoker	1-20 per day	21+ per day
Trichopolous et al (1981) (40 cases, 149 controls)	1.0	1.8	2.4	3.4
Trichopolous et al (1983) (77 cases, 225 controls)	1.0	1.9	2.4	3.4
Trichopolous et al (1983) corrected by Heller (1983) (77 cases, 225 controls)	1.0	1.9	1.9	2.5

Trichopolous data, one similar to that found by Hirayama: the non-smoking wives of heavy smokers were more likely to contract lung cancer than wives who actively smoked. Burch made the pointed comment: 'It is difficult to imagine that passive smokers - even with husbands smoking more than 20 cigarettes per day - could breathe in more carcinogens than active smokers'. There comes a point at which the case against passive smoking becomes too strong: it has been reached when evidence shows - or appears to show - that passive smoking is more dangerous than active smoking.

Trichopolous continued to add to his observations. By 1983 he had almost doubled his number of cases and controls. He published the results for the combination of new and old subjects and controls[17] *(Table 5)*. Remarkably, in spite of the increase, the risk-ratios were virtually unchanged: with ex-smoking husbands, 1.8 had become 1.9, with 1-20 cigarettes/day husbands the risk-ratio remained at 2.4, and for 21+ cigarettes/day husbands the risk-ratio remained at 3.4. Such resistance to change in the risk-ratios, though possible, is most unlikely and suggests there might be another explanation for the results. There is indeed, as Heller showed.[18] From the published data[19] Heller recalculated the ratios *(Table 5)*. Trichopolous replied to Heller 'He is right and we apologise for our typing error (which was pointed out by others including Dr Gosta Axelson of Goteborg, Sweden)'.[20] Once again, a rather casual response to a most serious criticism of the principal conclusion to his 1983 statement. Although published scientific results are normally taken on faith, such casualness in this case makes them at best questionable.

Despite errors Hirayama and Trichopolous studies still cited

In my opinion the results of Hirayama and Trichopolous have been vitiated both by the devastating criticisms which have been made of them and by the casual and indeed inadequate responses from their two authors.

How then have such august authorities as the Surgeon-General of the United States of America[21] and the National Health and Medical Research Council of Australia[22] arrived at the conclusion that the epidemiological evidence is 'strongly suggestive',[23] or 'compelling'?[24] The answer may lie in a quite uncritical evaluation of the evidence. Consider the results of Trichopolous. The NHMRC in its Report grasped the nettle firmly.[25] Only the original and incorrect calculations of risk-ratios given by Trichopolous et al[26] were quoted: no mention was made of the total recalculation of risk-ratios produced by Heller[27] and accepted by Trichopolous.[28] The Surgeon-General of the USA[29] gave the corrected values but attributed them to 'Trichopolous et al, 1983', where they do not appear, rather than to Heller who had corrected the faulty homework of Trichopolous et al. For his trouble, Heller does not even get mentioned by the Surgeon-General. This avoidance of published corrections leads to a quite natural sense of security in acceptance of erroneous published conclusions.

The results of Hirayama receive a similarly curious treatment. The Surgeon-General in a discussion of Hirayama's critics made no mention of the errors in Hirayama's 1981 paper. On the contrary, he said that in response to Lee's criticism 'the calculations were later confirmed'[30] but did not mention the fact that Hirayama himself admitted making errors of a magnitude which put them more in the realm of cosmology than epidemiology. The NHMRC Report on the other hand simplified the issue by not even mentioning the question of error.[31]

Other discredited studies also cited as fact

A similar lack of critical zeal has been effected with other papers on passive smoking. The study of Correa et al[32] is described in the NHMRC Report as showing 'Positive association in both males and females statistically significant'.[33] As shown by Correa et al, in their Table 1, it was in fact significant only for females. The Report also states that Correa et al, found a positive trend in lung cancer in non-smokers with passive smoking. They did not and nowhere say so. Garfinkel et al,[33] are described in the Report's Table 1 as having reported a 'Positive association in non-smoking females; statistically signficant'. Garfinkel et al in fact summarise their results by saying 'In conclusion, we found an elevated risk of lung cancer, ranging from 13 to 31 per cent, in women exposed to the smoke of others, although the increase was *not statistically significant'* (emphasis added). The justification for the Report's claim seems to be that the small subset of women whose husbands smoked more than 20 cigarettes per day were significantly more likely to develop lung cancer.[34]

The danger of such selective presentation of data is readily demonstrated: another subset of women, those who had been exposed to passive smoking for 1-2 hours per day over the last 25 years were significantly *less* likely to develop lung cancer.[35] It is possible to go through the multiple analysis of Garfinkel et al and find as many significant negative associations as positive associations but the overall result remains as stated by the authors and not by the NHMRC Report. Perhaps this discrepancy due to selective presentation is not surprising. The terms of reference of the NHMRC Committee required 'a thorough review of the literature'. Yet their Section 7, 'Passive smoking and cancer', in its 34-item bibliography includes no reference to Burch (1981), Heller (1983), Lee (1981), Mantel (1981), Rutsch (1981), Trichopolous (1984) or Hirayama's letters in response to criticisms levelled at his findings.

Passive smoking: no clear conclusions

It is evident from what has been presented that drawing a conclusion from the mass of published data on passive smoking and lung cancer is bound to be exceedingly difficult. One way of doing so is to consider the data at three successive levels of analysis. First, examine the results taken at face value. Second, examine the criticism of the work and the responses of the authors. Third, examine the reviews of experts.

At face value the published studies do little to inspire

confidence in anything stronger than a 'not proven' verdict, if not one of 'not guilty'. The great majority have produced no association between passive smoking and lung cancer. Any true correlation must be so small as to be scarcely detectable by even the most expensive and time consuming of trials.

The criticisms levelled at some of the most important studies have been both justified and convincing, and the responses of the authors have often been inadequate and inappropriate. It is in the nature of science that errors are made and published but few scientists make errors of the kind and order of those described here. There comes a point at which the most trusting reader, scientist or not, is justified in treating some published data with profound reserve.

It is the duty of experts whether in committee or not, critically to assess the evidence on which they will base their conclusions. That has not in general happened. Rather there has been what can only be described, and that generously, as selection and simplification. Even when the critical assessment and recalculation of the data have been done by others, the corrected amendments have been either ignored or incorporated without mention of the criticisms. Results have been selectively presented with untidy results left unpresented.

Ultimately, with the results presently available, any judgement must be subjective. But there is a way of obtaining a new perspective on the available material. Suppose the results described in this chapter referred not to cigarette smoke but to barbecue smoke wafted into a neighbour's backyard, or the vapour from deodorised family members and workmates. Would such results lead to the banning of barbecues or the exclusion of the deodorised from public society? The notion would, I think, be dismissed as absurd and resting on quite inadequate evidence, even though both meat smoke and deodorants may contain carcinogens.[36] But barbecues and the deodorised are not scapegoats. Not yet.

Life style and life expectancy: controlled trials versus circumstantial evidence

Hardly a day passes when the public are not given more advice on how to maintain and improve their health and live for a long time.

People should eat more fibre but less salt, fat, alcohol and nearly everything else. They should exercise more - but not if the sun is shining on them. Smokers must stop consuming tobacco even if giving up causes stress - which should also be avoided. Et cetera. The avalanche of advice is unending: but what does it mean overall? In principle it should be easy to find out: examine the mountain of evidence that accompanies the avalanche of advice. As might be expected, the practice is more difficult.

There are basically two kinds of evidence, circumstantial, and controlled trials. Circumstantial evidence can often be quite convincing by itself: The suicide who before your very eyes ingests strychnine and dies at your feet in convulsive agony is quite sufficient evidence to effectively prove the proposition that strychnine is a potent poison even in small quantities. On the other hand, the Prime Minister who assures us that it is the daily drink of his own urine which has preserved his health in his old age, puts up a less convincing case. He may be right, but we are much less inclined to drink urine for our health than we are to shun strychnine for our life.

But suppose we wanted to be very sure that urine did or did not improve health - it would, after all, be a very cheap tonic - how would we go about it? Perhaps we should examine the man concerned with careful medical attention. If it turned out that he had the body of a man 20 years older than himself, with terminal cancer of the pancreas and a heart on its last legs, then in spite of his protestations of good health we might be inclined to proceed no further. But if he had indeed the body of a 20 year old stripling instead, would this be sufficient evidence? No. His preternatural health could be due to any or all of a multitude of his other habits of a lifetime; perhaps the orange he ate religiously every night before going to sleep or his Vegemite on toast every Christmas. (Or none of them: if his centenarian father and grandfather came forward to condemn their offspring's dipsouria, we might suspect a good heredity as the cause of his good health.)

No, to find out as nearly as possible the truth about the beneficial effects of urine we would conduct a *controlled trial*. Take, say, a thousand healthy volunteers and divide them into two groups which are as similar as possible - age, weight, height, general health, etc. (Healthy individuals are employed even if at risk because of their 'unhealthy' life style. The ill constitute a different problem.) The 500 in the first group are then instructed to drink their own urine every morning. (Before volunteering this would have been put to them as a possibility they would have to face.) These people constitute the test group. The other 500 continue their lives as before and constitute a control group.

After, say, 10 years the two groups are compared to determine which contains the healthiest individuals. How is health to be assessed? There are many measures, but perhaps the best is death: the death rates (or the mean ages at death) in the two groups. Other measures are of value and interest but are less convincing. For example, 'feeling well' could be such a measure, but if the first group were all dead within a year, protesting to the last that they 'felt well', while the control group were all alive and 'feeling no different to before', the death rates would probably deserve more weight than the 'feel well' rates.

I have examined the circumstantial evidence concerning just two factors thought to be connected with health – blood cholesterol and exercise – in some detail. The controlled trials which have tested the effects of these and other risk factors were critically examined. Overall, these controlled trials have been well conducted so that a clear conclusion can be drawn from them: improvement in lifestyle and reduction of risk factors does not improve health. Struggle though they might, the proponents of a 'healthy' lifestyle must face this ineluctable conclusion. Struggle they have. The authors of these controlled trials have tried hard to support their hypotheses; statistical significance levels have been changed, trial endpoints have been changed, unsound statistical tests have been used, and, ultimately some have simply rejected their own findings. In spite of all, the results remain.

Changing medical fashions: attitudes to exercise

It is fascinating to observe the way medical fashions come and go. As a teenager, Pitt the Younger was prescribed a daily bottle of port wine for his gout.[37] Generations later, port was considered a certain *cause of gout*. Even tobacco has been considered a sovereign remedy and prophylactic:

Tobacco was then considered an excellent preservative against the plague, which committed dreadful ravages in the reign of Charles the Second; and the Eton boys were ordered to smoke in school daily. Tom Rogers told Hearne "that he was never whipped so much in his life as he was one morning for not smoking".[38]

As recently as 1942, a distinguished textbook recommended cigarettes as a preventive for asthma.[39]

Exercise, particularly strenuous exercise, is now widely regarded as beneficial to health and life expectancy. Yet during the first half of this century the converse was generally believed. Rook summarises the condition with a characteristically pithy Cambridge story:

How many regard what they consider to be the folly of undue exertion may be exemplified by the story of the elderly don, himself approaching his hundredth year, who deplored the death of a colleague some three years his junior with the remark that in his youth the dead man had been addicted to climbing mountains, and such exertions must unquestionably have shortened his life.[40]

Rook set out to determine whether exercise did indeed shorten life, an ironic state of affairs given the prevailing views 30 years later. Ideally, to answer that question the average age at death of a group of people who have exercised regularly throughout their lives should be compared with that of a matched, similar group who have not. Such an investigation of 70 or 80 years' duration is not practicable. Instead, Rook and later investigators assumed that a group of people who are voluntarily and vigorously active in their early life will be likely to continue to be more active than a similar group who enjoyed a more sedentary youth.

Rook examined the life expectancy of men who represented Cambridge University in sporting events during the years 1860 to 1900. He compared their mortality with that of honours graduates and that of 'non-sportsmen' and 'non-intellectuals' of the same period. The intellectuals lived longest with an average age at death of 69.41 years, then the sportsmen at 67.97 years and the random group at 67.43 years. Rook concluded

there was no evidence that the sportsmen died at an

earlier age than the group chosen at random; the intellectuals lived longer by a period averaging 1.5 years, but this
small difference might well be due to chance.

The difference might indeed have been due to chance but Rook,
though advised by the Cambridge medical school statistician
Dr W L Smith, did not bother to apply the usual statistical tests to
determine if this was the case. From his Table 4-III it seems that the
difference in favour of the intellectuals was not in fact significant. It
is important to note that Rook excluded deaths due to accident and
war but included suicide. For the intellectuals, 4.7 per cent of
deaths were due to accident or war injuries compared with 13.6 per
cent for athletes; for the intellectuals 4.1 per cent of deaths were
due to suicide compared with 0.9 per cent for the athletes. Since the
intention of the study was to determine the effects of early strenuous activity on the later condition of the body this selective inclu-
sion of one form of violent death (suicide) and exclusion of others
(accidents and war) seems odd. From the data Rook has provided it
is not possible to calculate with certainty the mean ages for non-
violent death in the different groups. In particular, Rook does not
state explicitly the number of suicides or their age at death. At best,
however, the sportsmen lived no longer than the intellectuals and
at worst their lives were significantly shorter.

Conclusion: medical science as promoter of a new puritanism

'The noblest work of man is the rational interrogation of nature and
the dispassionate analysis of nature's responses.' That or something less pompous, is how the average non-scientist might well
define science. By implication the scientist is a cool observer of the
universe, experimenting and ready to change his views to accom-
modate new data, his main goal being the pursuit of knowledge.
Although there is some truth in such a definition, the practising scientist knows there is much more to his craft. Practical science is
more like a competition in which the scientist attempts to outwit
both nature and his fellow scientists and emerge as the winner of a
great game. And to win the laurel scientists, whether great or
slight, have throughout history been prepared to take the
measures thought necessary. A prime example is Sir Isaac Newton's use of grossly unethical tactics to show that he, and not

Gottlieb Leibnitz, was the discoverer of the calculus. Newton's life is stained by his appalling treatment of his fellow scientists which surely reached its nadir with Leibnitz. Westfall sums up the wretched events:

> As President of the Royal Society, he appointed an 'impartial' committee to investigate the issue, secretly wrote the report officially published by the Society, and reviewed it anonymously in the Philosophical Transactions. Even Leibnitz's death could not allay Newton's wrath, and he continued to pursue the enemy beyond the grave. The battle with Leibnitz, the irrepressible need to efface the charge of dishonesty, dominated the final 25 years of Newton's life. It obtruded itself continually upon his consciousness. Almost any paper on any subject from these years is apt to be interrupted by a furious paragraph against the German philosopher, as he honed the instruments of his fury ever more keenly. In the end, only Newton's death ended his wrath.[41]

Few may behave with such extremity as Newton but his behaviour was more like that of an average scientist than our postulated cool observer of the universe. It is not surprising that scientists should be so. Like others, they require sustenance and seek recognition, yet the only means of achieving these objects is their ideas and results, their intellectual property. Such property is only of worth if it is original and that is why so much of research is nagged by the question of priority. When scientists collaborate, as has been usual for many years, the question becomes one of relative contribution and for the same reason. These undercurrents rarely come to the lay attention but when they do - as with the publication of J D Watson's *The Double Helix* - the public appear both surprised and amused by the discovery that scientists are human.

A consequence of the need to win is the temptation to cheat. Just as an athlete might take drugs to win a race, so a scientist might change his observations (or invent them) to obtain a predicted conclusion. The founder of genetics, Mendel, is thought to have falsified his observations because they are almost too good to be true or likely. There have been several notorious examples of fraud during the last ten years and this has caused some alarm in the scientific community. By its very nature, fraud is difficult to prove but there is a natural concern about its incidence. Unfortunately, practical science necessarily involves what amounts to fraud. There can be few if any scientists who have not discarded a result because the experiment 'went wrong'. This is deliberate suppression of an observation but without such filtering, progress would stop. (Here I think may be found the distinction between the great scientist and the rest. All strive to order the universe so that the world becomes a place of regular patterns with predictable future events. Discordant, ugly results will naturally tend to be discarded or overlooked. The great observer can distinguish between an ugly false result and an ugly true result and build substantially on the distinction. In T H Huxley's words, 'God give me strength to face an ugly fact though it slay me'.) The extent to which such filtering is permissible or even desirable very much depends on the particular instance and there can be no general answer.

So scientists may be both emotional and dishonest in ambitious defence of their intellectual property and most are so if only to a trivial degree. However, ambition does not appear adequate to account for the curious distortions of scientific data which have been described earlier. Another explanation must be found. The solution may lie in a common thread which joins all the examples I have given and many more that could be given. In every example, scientific method and results have been used as a weapon to deter people from enjoying themselves. Science has been prostituted to the cause of puritanism, the 'haunting fear that someone, somewhere, may be happy' (H L Mencken). Medicine has throughout history been conscripted in the cause of puritanism: certain acts and activities have been proscribed as both immoral and unhealthy. Indeed, it was because of their immorality that such acts were harmful. Masturbation, for example, was contrary to natural law and so produced 'masturbation insanity', a favourite illness of the Victorians. Food was always of particular interest. George Cheyne was an enormously popular 18th century physician whose reputation continued undiminished into the 19th century. In the many editions of his *An Essay of Health and Long Life* he expounded his view that the secret to a healthy, long life was an abstemious diet. This rested on his religious beliefs. God had shortened man's life after the deluge by the expedient of permitting him to eat meat, a food for which the human frame had not been designed. God was:

> obliged (that the Globe of the Earth might not, from the long lives of its inhabitants, become a Hell and a Habitation for incarnate Devils) to shorten their lives from 900 or 1,000 years, to 70. He wisely foresaw that animal food and artificial Liquors would naturally contribute towards this End; and indulged, or permitted, the Generation that was to start the Earth again after the Flood, the Use of these for Food; knowing that though it would shorten the Lives and plait a Scourge of Thorns for the Backs, of the Lazy and Voluptuous, it would be cautiously avoided by those who knew it was their Duty and Happiness to keep their Passions low, and their Appetites in subject.[42]

With God beside him, Cheyne was able to preach his medical ideas to the public with great success. Vegetables constituted the prudent diet, although even vegetables were a little suspect since they might contain insects and other small animals. Luckily, Cheyne was able to avoid a completely nutrition-free diet:

> But, besides what I have said, of Nature being quite altered and changed from what was originally intended, there is a great Difference between destroying and extinguishing an animal Life (which otherwise might subsist many Years) by Choice and Election to gratify our Appetites, and indulge Concupiscence; and the casual and unavoidable crushing of those who, perhaps otherwise, would die within the Day, or at most, the Year, and obtain but an inferior kind of Existence and Life at best.[43]

Quite apart from his theological views, the absurdity of his argument today seems transparent. If animal food is harmful to the body it should be so whether it is eaten accidentally or deliberately. In spite of this and many other inanities, he achieved enormous success and was widely regarded as one of the greatest physicians of his day, both in his lifetime (1671-1744) and for a century later. Curiously, Cheyne was prone to obesity, at one time weighing 32 stone (204 kg) and scarcely able to walk.

These are not aberrant examples in the history of medicine: moralising by medicalising permeates the fabric of the discipline from Hippocrates to the present (although Hippocrates is a detached observer with little to say about morality compared with many of his successors) a view which has been eloquently developed by Szasz.[44] As recently as 1942, Price's textbook of medicine, still esteemed in its more recent editions, pronounced nasal catarrh to be due to 'sexual excess and masturbation'.[43] It is not my purpose to here defend this thesis, except to suggest that doubters should simply browse through any pre-war textbook of medicine and see for themselves.

The reference to 'pre-war textbooks' implies that there has been a change during the past 40 years. That is indeed the case. God is out of fashion and old-fashioned morality is no longer considered sufficient medical reason to interfere with diet, sexuality or any other aspect of human behaviour. The wowsers[46] have been obliged to look elsewhere for justification. They have found it in a new morality which was expressed in a work of fiction *(Ligeia)* by Edgar Allan Poe: 'Man doth not yield himself to the angels nor unto death utterly, save only through the weakness of his feeble will'.

Our ill-health and death are our own fault. If we lived properly, that is, if we lived as the wowsers and puritans think we should, then we would live forever, or at least a very long time. That is the tacit morality which underpins much of modern medicine. The Heart Foundation declares it to be a scandal that so many people should die of cardiovascular disease, the cries of the Cancer Council are equally piteous over cancer deaths. (What *should* people die of?) It is not good enough that in Australia male life expectancy should be 72 years and female 78. The foundations of this secular morality are both shaky and changeable. The financial cost to the nation because of alleged premature death is sometimes mentioned. Sometimes it is the threat to others posed by smokers or drinkers. In fact there is scarcely any substance to this new morality. Wowserism is self-sufficient and self-justified.

We live in an age of superstition, the worse for being promoted as an age of enlightenment. Medical and scientific vandals have hijacked the tools and results of science and prostituted them to their own ends. Secure in the knowledge that the great majority of a deceived populace believe them, they have untrammelled freedom to persecute oppressed minorities. It is time for a change. Let those with an interest in public health and a sense of fair play examine the facts for themselves and draw their own conclusions.

Notes and references

1. Other diseases have been examined in this context but lung cancer has naturally received most attention and is the only one to be considered here.
2. K Diem (ed), *Documenta Geigy Scientific Tables*, St Leonard's NSW: Geigy Pharmaceuticals, 1962; R H Dreisbach, *Handbook of Poisoning: Diagnosis and Treatment*, Los Altos: Lange Medical Publications, 1977.
3. *Smoking and Health: Summary of a Report of the Royal College of Physicians of London on Smoking in Relation to Cancer of the Lung and Other Diseases*, London: Pitman, 1962, p.20.
4. T Hirayama, 'Non-Smoking Wives of Heavy Smokers Have a Higher Risk of Lung Cancer: A Study from Japan', *British Medical Journal*, 1, 1981, pp.183-185.
5. N Mantel, 'Non-Smoking Wives of Heavy Smokers Have a Higher Risk of Lung Cancer', *British Medical Journal*, 2, 1981, pp.914-915.
6. T Hirayama, 'Non-Smoking Wives of Heavy Smokers Have a Higher Risk of Lung Cancer', *British Medical Journal*, 2, 1981, pp.916-917.
7. M Rutsch, 'Non-Smoking Wives of Heavy Smokers Have a Higher Risk of Lung Cancer', *British Medical Journal*, 282, 1981, p.985.
8. T Hirayama, 'Passive Smoking and Lung Cancer', *British Medical Journal*, 282, 1981, pp.1393-1394.
9. P N Lee, 'Non-Smoking Wives of Heavy Smokers Have a Higher Risk of Lung Cancer', *British Medical Journal*, 283, 1981, pp.1465-1466.
10. Burch analysed a similar situation (P R J Burch 'Lifetime passive smoking and cancer risk', *The Lancet*, 1, 1985, p.866) which arose from the work of Sandler et al on all cancers (D P Sandler, A J Wilcox and R B Everson, 'Cumulative effects of lifetime passive smoking on cancer risk', *The Lancet*, 1, 1985, pp.312-315) and showed that there are three possible explanations for such a result: 1. active and passive smoking are both non-carcinogenic; 2. active smoking causes cancer and passive smoking prevents cancer; and 3. active smoking prevents cancer and passive smoking causes cancer.
11. A confidence interval is here an expression of the possible error in a measured risk ratio. For example a risk ratio of 3.0 may be the best available estimate, but if ten times as many cases had been examined a better estimate might have been obtained. Statistical techniques permit a range to be associated with the risk ratio, say 3 ± 1 (95 percent CI): in other words, we can be 95 percent certain that the risk ratio lies somewhere between 2 and 4.
12. T Hirayama, 'Non-Smoking Wives of Heavy Smokers Have a Higher Risk of Lung Cancer', *British Medical Journal*, 2, 1981, p.1466.
13. T Hirayama, 'Cancer Mortality in Non-Smoking Women with Smoking Husbands Based on a Large-Scale Cohort Study in Japan', *Preventive Medicine*, 13, 1984, pp.680.
14. D Trichopolous, A Kalondidi, L Sparros and B MacMahon, 'Lung Cancer and Passive Smoking', *International Journal of Cancer*, 27, 1981, pp.1-4.
15. For example, a risk ratio of 3 means that a passive smoker is 3 times more likely to get lung cancer than someone not thus exposed.

16. P R J Burch, 'Passive Smoking and Lung Cancer', *British Medical Journal*, 282, 1981, p.1393.
17. D Trichopolous, A Kalondidi, and L Sparros, 'Lung Cancer and Passive Smoking: Conclusions of a Greek Study', *The Lancet*, 2, 1983, pp.677-678.
18. W D Heller, 'Lung Cancer and Passive Smoking', *The Lancet*, 2, 1983, p.1309.
19. Trichopolous et al, 1983, op cit.
20. D Trichopolous, 'Passive Smoking and Lung Cancer', *The Lancet*, 24 March 1984, p.684.
21. C E Koop, *The Health Consequences of involuntary Smoking: A Report of the Surgeon-General*, US Department of Health and Human Services, 1986.
22. National Health and Medical Research Council, *Report of the Working Party on the Effects of Passive Smoking on Health*, 1986.
23. Ibid, p.38.
24. Koop, op cit, p.97.
25. National Health and Medical Research Council, op. cit. p.33.
26. Trichopolous et al, 1983, op cit.
27. Heller, op cit.
28. Trichopolous, 1984, op cit.
29. Koop, op cit, p.71.
30. Ibid, p.76.
31. National Health and Medical Research Council, op cit.
32. P Correa, L W Pickle, E Fontham, Y Lin and W Haensze, 'Passive Smoking and Lung Cancer', *The Lancet*, 2, 1983, pp.595-597.
33. L Garfinkel, O Auerbach and L Joubert, 'Involuntary Smoking and Lung Cancer: A Case-Control Study', *Journal of the National Cancer Institute*, 75, 1985, pp.463-469.
34. National Health and Medical Research Council, op cit. p.35.
35. L Garfinkel et al, op cit, Table 4.
36. H McGee, *On Food and Cooking*, New York: Charles Scribner's Sons, 1984; B Selinger, *Chemistry in the Marketplace*, Sydney, NSW: Harcourt Brace Jovanovich, 1989.
37. R Reilly, *William Pitt the Younger*, New York: Putnam, 1979.
38. H C M Lyte, *A History of Eton College (1440-1898)*, London, Macmillan, 1899.
39. F W Price (ed), *A Textbook of the Practice of Medicine*, London, Oxford University Press, 6th edition, 1942, p.1151.
40. A Rook, 'An Investigation into the Longevity of Cambridge Sportsmen', *British Medical Journal*, 1, 1954, pp.773-777.
41. R S Westfall, 'Sir Isaac Newton', article in *Encyclopaedia Britannica*, 15th edition, 1976.
42. C Cheyne, *An Essay of Health and Long Life*, London, 9th edition, 1745, p.93.
43. Ibid.
44. T Szasz, *The Theology of Medicine*, Baton Rouge, Louisiana: State University Press, 1977.
45. Price, op cit, p.1085.
46. 'A wowser is one who wants to compel everybody else...to do whatever he thinks right, and abstain from everything he thinks wrong', *OED* citing *Nation*.

7   Creative Statistics

Peter D Finch

Induction not to be confused with inducement

Induction is extrapolation from the particular to the general. While it is never certain, we often use it to explain things as, for example when we say, 'that accounts for it'. Such a claim is both an inducement to adopt a belief and an alleged induction from particular facts. Creative statistics is persuasive 'accounting for it': inducement masquerading as induction.

For example, to persuade you that exposure to a factor X is a danger you should avoid, I might tell you that your yearly risk of dying from a certain disease D is increased 15-fold if you habitually expose yourself to X. If you ask me to substantiate that claim, then I will tell you that of every 100,000 people like you, and similarly exposed to X, as many as 104 die annually from the disease D whereas of every 100,000 people like you, who are not exposed to X, as few as seven die from D each year. The relative increase in the number of deaths from D, viz. 104/7 is 14.9; this is the 15-fold increase of which I told you.

What I didn't tell you is that the same figures show that your annual chance of dying from D because of your exposure to X, when you would not have done so without that exposure, is just under one in 1,000, about the same as the chance of throwing 10 heads in a row with a fair coin.[1] An exposure risk as high as this may well make you think twice about exposing yourself to X. But giving it is not so persuasive an inducement to avoid X as is the more frightening figure of a 15-fold increase in risk. It would, perhaps, be even less frightening to be told that this exposure risk of about one in 1,000 corresponds to an annual chance of escaping death from D that is as much as 99.9 percent of that of a person not exposed to X.[2]

Absolute versus relative risk

These calculations illustrate how facts can be deliberately presented in different ways to evoke correspondingly different psychological responses. Health activists often present their argument in terms of relative risk to evoke fear as a response that will motivate us to adopt a lifestyle which they have deemed to be desirable for us. Does this matter? For if very many people each toss 10 coins, then about one in every 1,000 of them will turn up the dreaded 10 death-heads. The health activists' message is that this could be avoided and that this is so important that it justifies presenting the message as persuasively as possible by quoting the relative risk to emphasise the magnitude of the harmful effect in question. This justification raises issues that people react to in different ways according to whether they see themselves as educators or activists.

As I have documented elsewhere,[3] the overriding aim of the health activist is action to modify human behaviour. The aim of the health educator is to tell people what they need to know in order to make informed choices for themselves. The health activist has already made those choices for us and his or her primary aim is legislation to ensure that we abide by them. That is why some people see the individual's right to freedom of choice as a central issue. But, important as that issue is, it takes second place here to the question of whether the activists' claim that relative risk does measure the magnitude of a harmful effect is in fact correct. That it is not can be seen very simply and we shall do so by showing how a 10-fold reduction in relative risk can be associated with a doubling of the exposure risk. It is exposure risk, not relative risk, that measures the magnitude of the harmful effect of a factor; it is the risk of dying from a disease over the time period in question because of exposure to the factor, when you would not have died from it without the exposure.

In the illustrative example with which we started, the disease D was in fact ischaemic heart disease, the factor X was cigarette smoking and the figures given referred to men less than 45 years old who smoked 25 or more cigarettes per day. *Table 1* gives similar figures for other age groups, by the amount smoked. It shows that for male light-smokers aged 55-64 years the relative risk is only 1.4,

Table 1: Relative risk (RR) and exposure risk (ER) per thousand for ischaemic heart disease in males by age and current smoking[4]

Age (years)	Current smokers, smoking cigarettes only (no/day)					
	1-14		15-24		25+	
	RR	ER	RR	ER	RR	ER
<45	6.6	0.4	2.3	0.1	14.9	1.0
45-54	1.8	0.1	3.1	2.5	3.3	2.8
55-64	1.4	2.1	1.5	2.7	1.9	2.5
65-74	1.6	7.2	1.3	3.8	1.5	6.0
75+	1.1	2.5	1.0	<.1	1.3	7.5

a 10-fold reduction in the relative risk of 15 for youngest heavy-smoking group, but the exposure risk has doubled. The annual risk of dying from ischaemic heart disease, given that one would not have done so as a non-smoker, is now almost one in 500. This illustrates the fact that relative risk does not gauge harmfulness. What it does measure is the strength of the association between a disease and an exposure factor. A factor can be very strongly associated with a particular disease, so that almost all cases of the disease are due to the factor and the relative risk is very high, but still have only a small effect because the disease is rare even amongst those exposed to the factor.

Misuse of relative risk causes unnecessary worry over statistical trivia

It is not always clear whether some health activists simply do not understand that relative risk does not gauge harmfulness or whether they are deliberately fostering such a misinterpretation of the facts in order to persuade people to adopt their views. What does seem clear, however, is that the misuse of relative risk in that way has been central to the public campaign about the alleged harmful effects of other people's cigarette smoke. It is often said that non-smoking wives of smoking men have a 30 per cent increase in their risk of getting lung cancer. We will not discuss the many doubts that have been raised about the validity of the data on which that claim is based.[5] What we will discuss is the magnitude of the alleged harmful effect in question. The annual death rate from lung cancer among non-smoking wives of non-smoking men is of the order of six per 100,000. Among the non-smoking wives of smoking men the corresponding figure is eight per 100,000. Thus two in every 99,994 non-smoking wives of smoking husbands die of lung cancer that, it is claimed, should be attributed to the effects of passive smoking. This is an exposure risk of almost one in 50,000, about the chance of tossing 16 heads in a row. To put such a small exposure risk into perspective note that, in Australia, the death rate from injuries and poisonings for males aged 15-24 years, at 101 per 100,000, is about 50 times as great; whereas the male infant mortality rate, viz male deaths in the first year of life at 10 per 1,000 live births is 250 times as great. Similarly while light-smoking 55-64 year old men have a comparable 40 per cent increase in their annual risk of dying from ischaemic heart disease, their corresponding exposure risk at one in 500 is 100 times that alleged for lung cancer in non-smoking wives of smoking men. By emphasizing a 30 per cent increase in lung cancer due to passive smoking, health activists have led people to think that this is a high risk situation when that is not the case. Moreover it only makes sense to claim that there is a one in 50,000 annual exposure risk if we can measure annual disease-specific death rates that accurately in the data provided by the studies in question. It is arguable that we cannot do so. Errors in death certification are known to be higher than that and errors known to be associated with questionnaire-based data cloud the issue with further uncertainties. The most that one can say about the alleged link between passive smoking and lung cancer is that if there is one, then it is so small that it is difficult to measure it accurately and the risk, if any, is well below the level of those to which we normally pay attention.

Health activists bombard us with relative risks as if they were measures of harmfulness. Moreover they select the data and that part of the data which yield the biggest relative risks, apparently to induce us to adopt their beliefs; even though, as we have seen, smaller relative risks may be associated with greater harm. Clearly, whilst the fear of God is the beginning of wisdom, the fear of disease is not. Indeed one is forced to conclude that some health activists either lack a proper understanding of their subject or are being deliberately dishonest. Some people may find this conclusion outrageous because many health activists are also eminent medical authorities whose judgements are widely accepted without question. The underlying issue here is whether the medical profession is the only one, or even the correct one, to speak with authority on public health matters. Even to raise this as an issue is to go against established practice. But it is an issue that needs public discussion.

Medical experts not necessarily authorities in statistical interpretation

Many health matters resist elucidation except by the painstaking statistical analysis of many individual medical facts. One can be led astray not only by faulty analysis but also by faulty collection of material. It should neither surprise nor dismay us that such faults are common, because here, as in other areas of science, we progress by learning from our mistakes. Statistics is the sorting out of evidence from coincidence. First we must collect the data, deciding what to measure and how to measure it. In the health arena these are largely medical questions, but they also include design issues of a purely statistical nature. Medical authority rightly decides what are the relevant medical facts and it rightly decides what broad aspects of those facts are important to medicine. But at that stage medical authority ends because the determination of what a large body of medical facts is telling us is not itself a medical problem, even when the individual facts are medical ones. It is a statistical problem. Of course there is nothing in principle to stop a medical authority from being a statistical authority also. Some of them are. But the appeal to medical authority per se to decide evidential issues in large bodies of medical facts is entirely without substance.

This issue of medical authority arose recently in the Federal Court of Australia in a case involving the Trade Practices Act. It concerned a statement in an advertisement authorised by the Tobacco Institute.[6] That statement said, inter alia, '...There is little evidence and nothing which proves scientifically that cigarette smoking causes death in non-smokers'. The judge found against the Tobacco Institute and asserted that there is evidence proving that cigarette smoke causes disease in non-smokers. A careful reading of the judgement and the reasons for it reveal the positively mediaeval way in which the judge interpreted the term 'evidence'. He said, '...The opinions of competent experts on a matter falling within their field of expertise may afford grounds for belief as to that matter. Many...would understand such opinions to be evidence relevant to the question whether cigarette smoke causes disease in non-smokers'. The judge clearly considered the epidemiologists appearing before him as the experts and was not impressed by the statisticians, who, he seemed to feel, were so cautious that they would never reach a firm conclusion about anything. He relied almost entirely, it seems on the self-proclaimed authority of the medical experts and clearly interpreted the relative risks they presented as measures of harmfulness.

Many people are like this Federal Court judge, they believe that firm conclusions are out there, waiting to be grasped, if only we can work our way through to them, and that cautiousness is an occupational idiosyncrasy of statisticians that is best ignored by practical men and women. Statisticians are cautious. Indeed you can always identify the statistician amongst a group of scientists by looking for the one who is boasting about how much he or she does *not* know. For the statistician the odd thing is that so many people are sure that complex problems have well-defined unique solutions, that scientists are the people to find them and that, as noted by C P Snow in his essay *Science and Government*, 'Even at the highest level of decision, men do not really relish the complexity of brute reality, and they will hare after a simple concept whenever one shows its head'.

Scientific objectivity threatened by politicisation

There are always scientists ready to take advantage of this situation by pointing to political gains associated with the official adoption of their particular theories. This is a well-known part of the cultural milieu of science. But it is seldom recognised openly that scientific research is directed not only to the advancement of knowledge but also to the advancement of status and professional standing. It is less disturbing to popularise the belief that good science is depersonalised and objective, that grant-sponsored academic research is prejudice-free whereas commercially-sponsored research, particularly in the health arena, is contaminated by profit-motivated bias. The real world of science is not like that. In thirty or so years of statistical consulting, mostly to academic scientists, I have not had even one objective client. Each of them has had a prior conviction that something is the case and the experiment in question was performed to confirm it. The approach is invariably, 'how can I use these results to prove my theory?' This is not necessarily a bad thing. It is simply the way scientists are motivated. Scientific objectivity is not about the motivation for doing research, nor the source of its funding, it has to do with the criteria by which we assess it. But these criteria are being eroded by the politicisation of science, especially in matters of health.

Health activists have contributed to this erosion of scientific standards by adopting the Lalonde doctrine that 'action has to be taken even if all the scientific evidence is not in'.[7] In pursuit of that aim, they have fostered, and encouraged the media to adopt, the view that publication per se is the scientific seal of approval. But publication in a professional journal is only the first step towards scientific accreditation. It is the way scientists present their findings for scrutiny by the scientific community and, hopefully, eventual incorporation into the discipline in question. This is a slow process. Inter alia, it involves reproducibility by other workers in diverse circumstances and the unfolding of the relationship between the new findings and what is already known. A journal's reviewing procedures aim to do little more than select for publication those findings, amongst the many submitted to it, for which such scrutiny seems to be particularly worthwhile. Many journal articles are then, in effect, little more than a suggestion that something one did is interesting and important enough for other people to investigate to see if the findings do extrapolate to the general run of things. But health activists are apt to seize upon such tentative findings as soon as they appear in print, at least when they seem to support their general purposes, and report them as if they were established scientific truths. This has a number of deleterious effects. Firstly the public is given a distorted view of current scientific research because there is no public advocacy of the findings that do not support the activist's beliefs and the favoured scientists are likely to welcome any endorsement of their work. Secondly tentative findings are presented as benchmark truths even when other studies do not confirm them. A typical example is the way health activists repeatedly emphasise the early findings on the possibility of a link between passive smoking and lung cancer at the expense of later studies which did not confirm them.[8] Finally they promote a cultural climate in which complicated problems are expected to be rapidly resolved in simple ways by spending more and more on scientific research.

Seldom only one possible solution to any complex problem

Since Gödel, educated people have come to accept the idea that within an axiom system there may be certain problems which are inherently unsolvable within that system. But it does seem to be generally appreciated that an inductive version of unsolvability pervades the whole field of unravelling complex situations. Any way of talking about data, in other words talking about the world itself, involves the adoption of a certain type of model of the world. When scientists use statistics they restrict themselves to certain types of model then fashionable within the current paradigm of enquiry within their science. Statistical analysis enables them to present one of those models as the one that best fits the facts. But at a deeper level the statistician can always formulate other models that fit the facts just as well. In other words there are always other explanations, sometimes bizarre, usually unfashionable and seldom considered by scientists, or their consulting statistician for that matter. But the statistician knows that there are other complex mathematical models that would fit the facts. Much as one would like to adopt Occam's razor and rule them out, he or she is aware that some of them could turn out to be better models of reality than the ones now in use. In a very real sense, then, little about the structure of the world can be established with great certainty. Some things can be disproved by observation but they can seldom, if ever, be proved. We should, then, guard ourselves against those who claim to have the solution to complex problems. What they have is often only the solution suggested by a model of reality that fits the facts. In general there will be other models that fit the facts just as well and might suggest different solutions.

Creative statistics includes not only selecting the facts to suit one's case and presenting them in the most advantageous way to silence opposition and induce others to adopt one's point of view, it is also based on the idea that one's perception of the world is the only correct one. Particularly in matters of human behaviour, whether it be religious observance, lifestyle or political organisation, there are always those who think that God blundered when he gave us free-will and seek to rectify that by limiting the choices available to us.

Notes and references

1. Of the 99,993 = 100,000 - 7 people who do not die of D when unexposed to X, 97 = 104 - 7 do die of D when that group is exposed to X. The annual chance of dying from D when exposed to X is then 94/99,993, just under 1/1000. The chance of throwing 10 heads in a row with a fair coin is 1/1024.

2. The chance that a person escapes death from D is (100,000 - 7)/100,000 or (100,000 - 104)/100,000 according as he or she is or is not exposed to X. The ratio of the second to the first is one minus the exposure risk calculated in note 1, viz about 0.999.

3. P D Finch, 'The Lalonde Doctrine in Action: The Campaign Against Passive Smoking', *Policy*, Winter 1990, pp.22-25.

4. Calculated from Table 2.11 of N E Breslow and N E Day, *Statistical Methods in Cancer Research*, Vol.1., Lyons: International Agency for Research on Cancer, 1980.

5. Peter N Lee, *Misclassification of Smoking Habits and Passive Smoking*, Berlin: Springer-Verlag, 1988: D J Ecobichon and J M Wu (eds.), *Environmental Tobacco Smoke*, Proceedings of the International Symposium at McGill University 1989, Lexington, USA: D C Heath and Co, 1990; J R Johnstone and C Ulyatt, *Health Scare*, Australian Institute of Public Policy, 1991.

6. Federal Court of Australia, New South Wales District Registry General Division. No. G253 of 1987.

7. Finch, op cit.

8. See note 5.

8 A Healthy Diet – Fact or Fashion?

James Le Fanu

The Western diet cannot be both 'healthy' and 'unhealthy'

Common sense dictates that the prevailing nutritional beliefs about the harm of our Western 'high fat' diet must be wrong. We live in a society where for the first time in history most people live out their biological life span to die from diseases strongly determined by ageing - those of the circulatory system and cancer. If the Western diet has played an important role in prolonging society's longevity (of which there can be no doubt) it cannot in the same breath be denounced as a cause of the age-related diseases that people die from as a consequence.

But the trouble with common sense, as Voltaire observed, is that it is not very common so sceptics like ourselves have to look elsewhere for appropriate arguments. Perhaps nutritional wisdom is merely another fad or fashion. Certainly over the last 100 years each component of the human diet – carbohydrate, protein and fat – has at different times been incriminated as harmful or promoted as being uniquely beneficial.

However the prevailing nutritional wisdom is much more than a mere fashion. Beliefs about the harmful nature of the Western diet have been around for the best part of 20 years. They have been endorsed by countless expert committees, are believed in and promoted by virtually every doctor, and in popular culture they have the same status of self evident veracity as the common belief that smoking is harmful to health.

Nonetheless I want to show how given a sufficient historical perspective, an examination of the scientific evidence that underpins the two main contradictory nutritional wisdoms of the last 50 years shows that fashion does indeed play an important role.

Nutritional guidelines have been reversed in one generation

From the 1930s onwards for 30 years to the mid 1960s a 'healthy diet' was high in fat, low in fibre. High fat foods such as milk, meat and dairy products were promoted as being 'protective' because they protected against disease while carbohydrate based foods full of fibre - bread, pasta, potatoes - were dismissed as being starchy and therefore fattening.

From the mid 1960s onwards this version of the healthy diet has been turned on its head. A healthy diet is now low in fat and high in fibre. Meat, milk and dairy products are deemed to be harmful because their high saturated fat content makes them a cause of heart disease, cancer, stroke and so on, while carbohydrate based foods, high in fibre, are promoted as protecting against these diseases as well as diabetes, varicose veins and cancer of the colon. There has been no dramatic revolution in the nutritional sciences to explain this change of heart, so we have closely to examine their sources.

The ideology of nutrition

The ideological climate of the 1930s was, as we all know, dominated by the depression, large scale unemployment, poverty and class conflict which it was widely believed capitalism could not resolve. It was an opportune time to argue that changes or improvements in diet might help those whom the political system had so obviously failed.

At this point John Boyd Orr, later Lord Boyd Orr and winner of the Nobel Peace Prize, Director of the Rowett Nutritional Institute outside Aberdeen in Scotland, enters the picture to argue that a high fat diet is a healthy diet. The evidence for this contention can be summarised in a graph which shows that upper class school children educated at Christ's Hospital were on average taller than those of working class children educated at State schools.[4] (See *Fig 1*)

This height differential Boyd Orr attributed, quite rightly, to the fact that boys at Christ's Hospital had a relatively higher fat diet with more meat, milk and dairy products than those of working class children who in turn could be said to have failed to fulfil their optimal height potential. If height attainment was used as a criteria

Figure 1: Heights of schoolchildren by social class

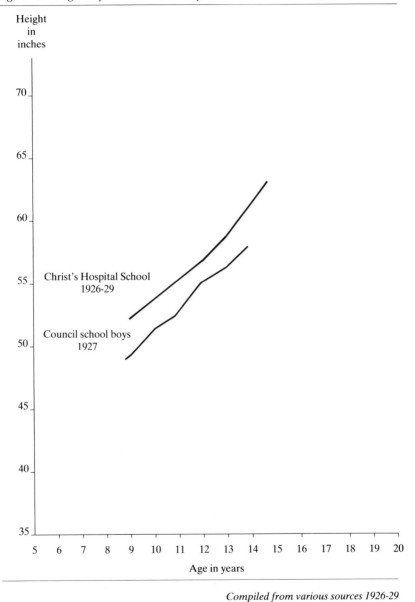

Height
in
inches

70

65

60

55 — Christ's Hospital School
1926-29

Council school boys
50 — 1927

45

40

35

5 6 7 8 9 10 11 12 13 14 15 16 17 18 19 20

Age in years

Compiled from various sources 1926-29

of a good diet then clearly the higher the fat content the better. Fair enough.

Sir John Boyd Orr and many politicians however went further than this to argue that the height discrepancy also indicated a health discrepancy claiming that large sections of the working class were chronically under-nourished and as a consequence in poor health. Thus during a typical debate in the House of Commons in 1936 on 'the growing evidence of widespread malnutrition...and the continued failure of Her Majesty's Government to take effective steps to deal with the unjust problem of hunger and want in the midst of plenty', Sir John Boyd Orr's studies were cited as showing 'there were nine million people in the country whose diet was defective in "protective" constituents'.

In this political climate it is not surprising it soon became self evident that the diet of the wealthy was 'healthier' than that of the poor. In fact a detailed physical examination of many children across the social classes done in 1938 failed to reveal any marked discrepancies in health: working class children were smaller certainly but there was no difference in the incidence of anaemia, rickets, vitamin deficiencies and so on.

The ideology of nutrition: the 1960s

We now move fast forward to the mid 1960s to find the world changed beyond recognition. Capitalism has triumphed, bringing undreamt of levels of prosperity across all social classes. All would seem to be well except for the fact that an apparently new disease was sweeping across the nation killing thousands of men prematurely - Coronary Heart Disease. Almost unknown in the mid 1920s this disease had increased exponentially in incidence year on year to become the commonest form of premature death in males. What could be the cause?

There were several possible candidates notably some mechanism causing thrombosis in the coronary arteries but one theory came to dominate all - the culprit was a high fat diet which, it was alleged, resulted in cholesterol infiltrating the walls of the arteries to the heart. This imagery of fat on the plate entering the blood to be laid down on the arteries was immensely potent.

There was some circumstantial evidence to support this theory (particularly the observation that Japanese with their low fat diet had a low rate of heart disease), which I will later show to be meaningless, but for the moment I will only point out that as soon as it became widely accepted a low fat diet might prevent coronary

Figure 2: The rise and fall of heart disease 1950-1980 compared with changes in fat consumption

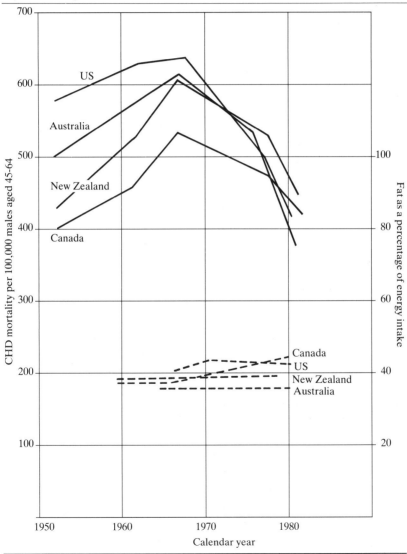

heart disease this then became the 'new healthy diet'. From the early 1970s onwards this new nutritional wisdom gained widespread acceptance, much strengthened by a precipitate fall in coronary heart disease which was attributed to widespread changes to a 'healthy life style' and notably a reduction of fat intake in the diet. This is obviously very important and to examine it further I now turn to the second graph which is the changing pattern of premature coronary heart disease in four countries - Australia, New Zealand, the United States and Canada between 1950 and 1985 (see *Fig 2*). As you will see, in each of these countries apparently simultaneously coronary heart disease rose precipitously year on year to peak in the mid 1960s, since when it has declined with equal rapidity. One could extrapolate this graph backwards to the mid 1930s when heart disease was first recognised as an important cause of premature death in men and then forwards which allows us to predict that it will cease to be an important health problem in the early part of the next century.

No simple relationship between fat consumption and heart disease

There are several vital points that arise from *Fig 2*. First it is not the pattern of a disease powerfully influenced or determined by social habits. If it were, it would presuppose that not just in one but several countries simultaneously everyone in the 1920s and 1930s started leading an unhealthy life style - smoking, taking little exercise, eating much more fat (to explain the initial rise in the disease) and then sometime in the 1950s these social habits changed and everybody started smoking less, eating less fat and taking more exercise (to explain the subsequent decline).

Further such changes in social habits would have had to have occurred across all age groups and all classes as the rise and fall of heart disease has occurred in all sections of society. Not only is there no evidence of this, (and I will turn to that in a minute), but it defies common sense.

Finally, we turn to examine the data on fat consumption during this period also shown in *Fig 2*. Now, to begin to explain the changing pattern of heart disease in terms of the conventional understanding of the influence of fat consumption on cholesterol levels would have required truly massive changes in fat intake rising from around 12 per cent of energy intake (as found in Japan) to 40 per cent (as found in the West) and then subsequently to have fallen back again to around 20 per cent to 30 per cent. No such changes have occurred. To be sure there have been changes in the consumption of certain visible fats notably a fall in consumption of butter, milk and eggs but these have been more than compensated for by a rise in meat consumption.

In essence the dietary patterns of societies tend to be remarkably stable and over the last 100 years that of the Western world has been dominated by dairy farming with relatively little fish and stable consumption of cereals. There have been changes, but the point is they have been both too small in magnitude and certainly have occurred too late to explain the striking change in the pattern of heart disease.

My conclusion from *Fig 2* is that coronary heart disease must primarily be an unexplained biological phenomenon in which fat consumption or a high cholesterol level (caused by defective genes) and cigarette smoking may have an additional but not determinant role. Of course the reason why this is not generally appreciated is that the data I have discussed are never presented in this way. Put bluntly, the facts have been selected and edited, preventing their proper interpretation and it is not surprising that when we turn to the circumstantial evidence that is held to underpin the relationship between a high fat diet and heart disease we find it has been similarly edited. The two crucial pieces are the comparison between countries of fat in the diet and the level of heart disease - the so called 'cross cultural' comparisons of which the classic is that of Ancel Keys. The second are the 'migrant studies' where the changing pattern of heart disease has been examined predominantly in Japanese migrating from Japan to the United States.

Despite their apparent simplicity, cross cultural studies are deeply ambiguous

Cross cultural studies can be said to have started off the diet heart disease story. The image they convey is a potent one. On one extreme are the thin, wiry Japanese with little fat in their diet and little coronary heart disease and at the other we have obese, high fat consuming, western men with a high incidence of coronary heart disease. But within the countries of Western Europe there is an enormous discrepancy between the incidence of heart disease for a very similar level of fat consumption - almost five fold between France and Finland. This is shown in *Fig 3*.

Figure 3: International comparisons of fat consumption and incidence of heart disease

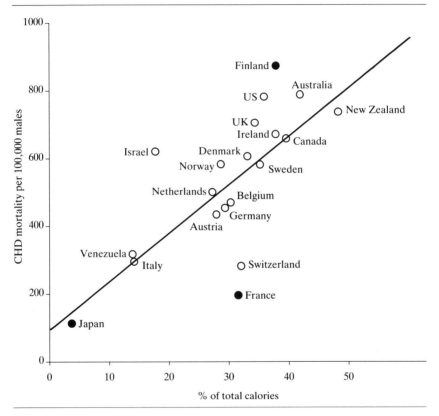

When similar countries are compared (France and Finland) there is no relationship between the amount of meat and dairy products consumed (as a percentage of total calories in the diet) and the rate of heart disease.

What the cross cultural studies appear to show is a biological dose-response relationship between the amount of fat in the national diet and the level of coronary heart disease based on an assumption that disparate societies have a similar susceptibility to any given cause of disease. In other words if X consumption of fat causes Y amount of heart disease in Japan then 2X amount of fat consumption in Finland would cause 2Y amount of heart disease in Finland. If this assumption were correct then one should be able to show a similar cross cultural relationship between a known cause and effect phenomenon, that is between smoking and lung cancer. But we cannot. There is a massive difference in mortality from lung cancer between Mexico and the United Kingdom for almost the same level of cigarette smoking, as can be seen from *Fig 4*.

However, if we look at a 'within-cultural' comparison comparing societies of roughly similar cultural and genetic composition, like Northern Europe, we can indeed show an apparent dose-response relationship (see *Fig 5*). The low levels of cigarette smoking in Iceland are rewarded with low levels of lung cancer rates and higher cigarette consumption in the United Kingdom is associated with high cancer rates. Why should this be?

Interestingly Keys' cross cultural comparison provides the answer. Amidst all the data he produced he showed that within the broad groups of the countries of Northern and Southern Europe there is a relationship between the amounts smoked and lung cancer rates but the actual incidence of lung cancer between the two cultures is very different (see *Fig 6*).

Now one could speculate why this might be the case - perhaps the Southern Europeans are protected by their genes or by something in their diet - but for the moment that does not matter. The crucial point is that it shows the assumption (in retrospect obviously) that different countries have the same susceptibility to a given cause of disease must be false.

The necessary corollary of this is that only a comparison of countries with a similar culture can be used to demonstrate a genuine cause-effect relationship, cross cultural comparisons cannot. Returning to our comparison of fat consumption and heart disease between countries, the apparent evidence of a dose-response relationship as shown by the differing rates in Japan and Finland

HEALTH, LIFESTYLE AND ENVIRONMENT

Figure 4: Cigarette consumption and lung cancer across countries I

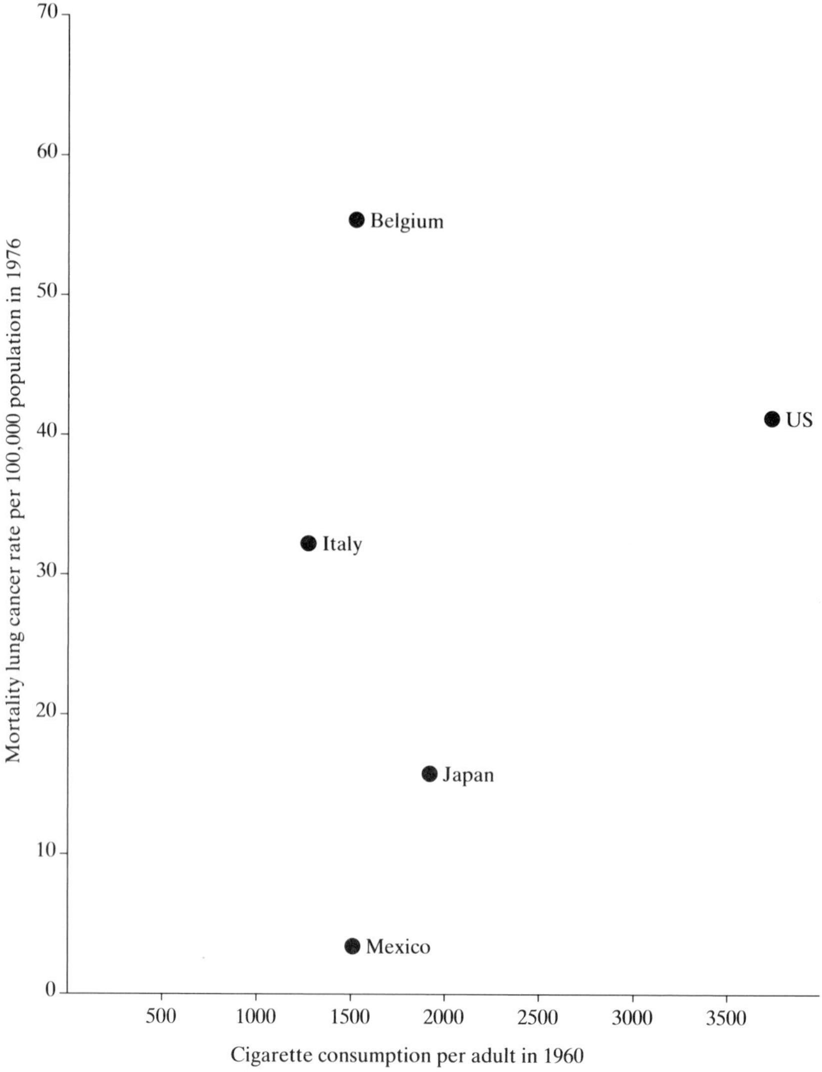

There is no relationship between cigarette smoking and death rate from lung cancer between countries.

96

Figure 5: Cigarette consumption and lung cancer across countries II

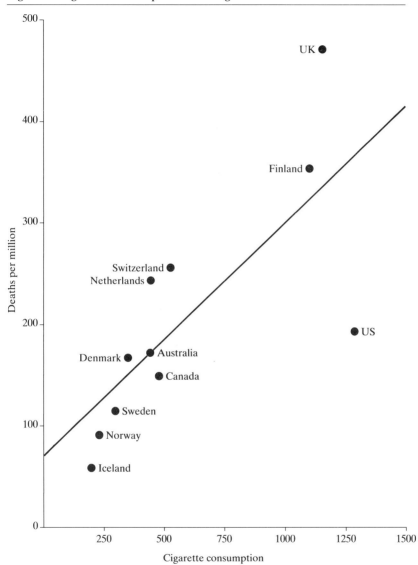

When similar countries are compared there is a relationship between cigarette smoking and the death rate from lung cancer.

Figure 6: Cigarette consumption and lung cancer III

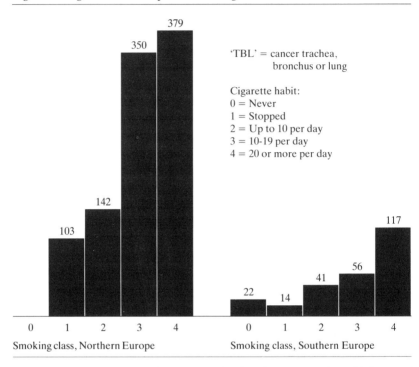

'TBL' = cancer trachea, bronchus or lung

Cigarette habit:
0 = Never
1 = Stopped
2 = Up to 10 per day
3 = 10-19 per day
4 = 20 or more per day

Smoking class, Northern Europe

Smoking class, Southern Europe

Within both Northern and Southern Europe the risk of lung cancer rises with increased cigarette smoking. But the risk is much greater in Northern Europe.

must then be rejected as invalid, while the evidence that heart disease rates are not related to fat consumption (as demonstrated by the within cultural comparison of France and Finland) must be considered as valid.

Evidence from migrant studies equally ambiguous

The Japanese migrant studies are presented as confirmatory evidence of the observation of the cross cultural studies. Here again we have an image of the Japanese moving to the United States adopting a high fat diet and as a consequence keeling over from heart disease (see *Fig 7*).

Figure 7: Rate of heart disease among Japanese in Japan and the US

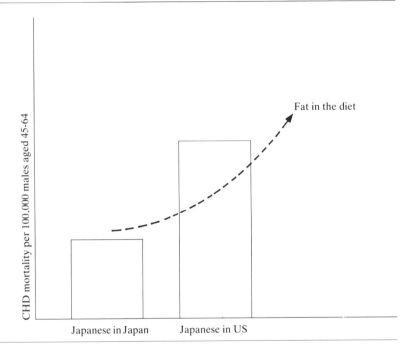

The rate of heart disease increases in Japanese migrants to the United States as they increase the amount of fat in their diet.

However if we look at other migrant studies we see this deduction is at least questionable. The Swedes have similar levels of fat consumption compared to the United States but lower heart disease rates. When Swedish migrants moved to the United States their heart disease rates doubled even though the amount of fat in their diet remained the same. (Sèe *Fig 8.*)

Figure 8: Rate of heart disease among Swedes in Sweden and the US

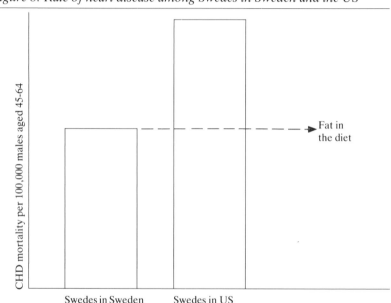

The rate of heart disease increases in Japanese migrants to the United States as they increase the amount of fat in their diet.

This observation requires further examination of the changing pattern of disease in migrants and here we find there is a generalised phenomenon that migrants lose the patterns of disease of their native country and acquire those of their adoptive country. Thus the rates of common Japanese diseases like stomach cancer and stroke fall as Japanese migrants move to the United States while low incidence diseases like heart disease and breast cancer rise to the levels that are found in their adoptive country. (See *Fig 9.*)

Figure 9: Changing incidence of diseases in Japanese migrants to the US

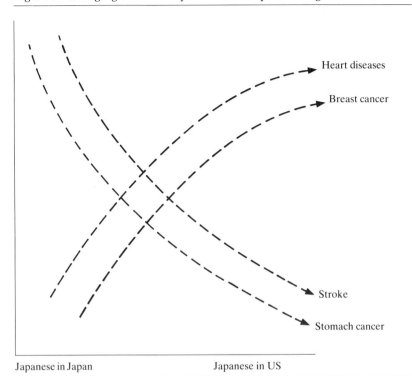

Heart diseases

Breast cancer

Stroke

Stomach cancer

Japanese in Japan   Japanese in US

Now diet may play a role in this but the point is that the heart disease experience of the Japanese migrants is presented as specific evidence of a direct relationship between fat consumption and heart disease where in fact it is only one instance of a much more generalised phenomenon.

Conclusions: changing nutritional fads reflect more general changes in perceptions

I have examined the circumstantial evidence in some detail to show what we have already seen from looking at the changing pattern of heart disease, that those responsible for promoting the diet-heart disease theory seem to me to have deliberately edited or censored evidence to justify their case. The facts are not in dispute, it is just the context within which they have been presented is misleading. Would the cross cultural comparisons of fat consumption and heart disease be generally accepted if it were widely known that such a relationship does not hold for such a classic cause-effect relationship as that of smoking and lung cancer? Would we accept the evidence of the Japanese migrant studies if it were also widely known that a similar effect occurs in the Swedes whose fat consumption does not change on moving to the United States?

And this takes me back to my starting point. We can properly talk about fashions in nutritional wisdom if we can show they rely on a partial presentation of facts that strikes a chord with prevailing ideological beliefs. Now though the two fashions in nutritional wisdom of the last 50 years are self evidently contradictory - a high fat diet cannot possibly move from being 'healthy' to 'unhealthy' within such a short period of time, nonetheless they share a lot in common and can be analysed in terms of how fashionable ideas are generated and then take hold. Both evoked a semantic description of meat and dairy foods that powerfully pre-judged their presumed benefit or harm. In the 1930s they were 'protective' foods because they protected against disease. In the 1960s they carried the sinister title of being 'high in saturated fats'. Both evoked powerful imagery of the role of food in health to explain suggested mechanism of disease. First it was that a relative deficiency of 'flesh and bone forming' meat and dairy foods explained a presumed state of chronic ill health amongst the working class. Then in the 1960s fat was believed to 'fur up the arteries'.

That much seems clear, but why did these nutritional wisdoms take root and flourish so vigorously at the times they did? Their popularity and acceptance cannot be explained on the basis that the public were impressed by the subtlety of the scientific arguments. More probably they touched deeper polarities of perception within society. At its simplest the 1930s enthusiasm for high fat meat and dairy food draws on 'high church' values, the 1960s rejection of these same foods draws on low church values of asceticism and egalitarianism.

And here we come to the rub. Nutritional wisdoms about healthy diet are utopian, their attraction is that they fulfil the need of individuals and societies to improve themselves. The utopian response to the depression of the 1930s was to demand that all should embrace the nutritional habits of the upper class with a diet high in dairy foods. The utopian response to the affluence of the 1960s is based on the supposition that prosperity is harmful and that harm can be mitigated by an ascetic diet that spurns high fat foods in favour of cereals, fibres, bread and pasta.

9   Reactions to Health and Environmental Risks: Reason versus Reflex

Mark Mills

Exaggerated health care fears are distorting public policy

People worry about their health, and about potential insults to it. Thus environmental risks that have a potential or theoretical health impact are understandably worrisome and the subject of considerable media attention and public confusion. The prevalence of misunderstandings and belief in outright mythology regarding health threats from environmental factors causes serious distortions in public policy. Policies intended to make lives less risky often do not, and the failure is frequently attended by great financial and emotional costs.

To understand human nature is to be able to manipulate it

The literature is filled with examples of public misperceptions of risks. Illuminating specific health and environmental issues and policies is a frequent topic of workshops and symposia. Here, rather than itemize the specific examples of distortions and misperceptions, I propose to explore the structural reasons that cause these distortions to occur in the first place. Understanding this says a lot about why they occur, and also how they can be manipulated.

When people understand how distortions in perceptions occur, they learn how to change or manipulate them, both for better or worse. This is how soothsayers and fortune tellers operate. They understand how people process information, what they like to hear and successfully manipulate people into believing things that are outright nonsense. This is also the process by which social engineers operate in their attempts to manipulate public policy. These latter, however, operate on a far grander scale. Their primary vehicle is the media, for obvious reasons. It has been robustly demonstrated that most people, including the highly educated, get most of their information on most subjects from the media – and primarily the electronic media.

The divergence between public and expert perceptions of risk

Experts and the public do not agree on what poses the most serious risks to public health. A 1990 Roper and Environmental Protection Agency (EPA) study on risk found a tremendous divergence between the opinions of experts and those of the public. A list of 28 different risks was evaluated by 75 risk experts and ranked in order of seriousness. A public poll on the same risks was conducted by Roper. Not only did the two rank orderings not agree, but the rankings appeared to be virtually reversed. There was, in short, an inverse correlation between the real threat of environmental risks and public perceptions of those risks. The study found, however, a close correlation between the public ranking and media attention afforded the risks. In other words, the more attention devoted to the risk, the more the public perceived the risk as a serious threat to themselves; a not particularly surprising but important validation.

An earlier (1988) related study performed at Rutgers University (New Jersey) found similar results. The study evaluated 564 media stories on environmental risks covered by the three major U.S. television networks (ABC, CBS, NBC) and compared the media content to the expert consensus on the same topics. Again, an inverse correlation was found. The media focused the most attention on the risks that were evaluated by experts as the least worrisome.

One should not be surprised, therefore, to find that national polls reveal 80 per cent of the public believe life is riskier today than 20 years ago. The problem of misperceptions or delusions about risks is serious in that it distorts how public funds are spent in the attempt to make us feel safer and healthier. It is well documented that public spending – evaluated in perhaps the only possible common denominator, dollars spent per actual or theoretical life saved – varies on average ten to one hundred fold and occasionally as much as a million fold. (See for example Mendeloff and Kaplan, State University of New York.) Highway safety measures, for example, frequently fall in the range of $10,000 per life saved spent in improvements. At the other end of the spectrum, for instance, is nuclear waste disposal where public expenditures per life saved reach one billion dollars. The large divergences in effective funding among public health policies causes, risk experts note, squandering of public funds and arguable loss of life where money could have been more sensibly directed.

Public money should not be spent on equalising risks

Some analysts, in considering the dichotomy between how we spend money on what we worry about and what really causes health risks, imply or assert that the policies should be linear. That is, everything that causes a one in a million chance of death should have the same dollar value placed on its reduction. This is an unachievable and overly restrictive view. For an imaginary example, the facts might demonstrate that there is a theoretical one in a million chance of death from polyvinyl chlorides in drinking x gallons of liquid from plastic bottles, and that there is also a one in a million chance of death from six minutes of canoeing, and that there is also a one in a million chance of death from radiation exposure resulting from living next to the Three Mile Island nuclear power plant at the time of the accident. Even though these three risks are statistically comparable, it is both unlikely and ill-advised to believe that public policies could result in equal expenditures in controlling the risks from each of them.

Many studies have documented the different valuation that people place on different kinds of risks to their health. People are more afraid of cancer than of drowning, and are comfortable with the idea that more should be spent reducing the former rather than the latter risk. However, people, when asked, are not prepared to accept (if they know about it) wildly divergent expenditures, which is the case with many current and proposed public health policies. One study of people's evaluations of the acceptable differences in risk-reduction expenditures found variations of twofold, and occasionally several fold identified as tolerable. Yet the facts show that policies now in effect in many countries have cost discrepancies of several hundred fold. It is likely that the distortions in public spending on health risks are greatly influenced by serious distortions of perceptions of the magnitude of those risks.

The media have a responsibility for distorting public perceptions of risk

The distortions in public perceptions of risk arise because of two structural factors: the nature of the media and the manner in which people process information. I am ignoring here distortions that are deliberately created for reasons of ideology or politics, not because these factors are not real and serious. But, the issues of motivations deliberately to distort risk are different in character. More to the point, those who have reasons to distort perceptions are successful in doing so when they understand the structural mechanisms that lead to misperceptions. In other words, there is an underlying structural reality; as Irving Kristol says elsewhere in this book, the underlying nature of how we perceive risk information is not a problem, it is a condition. It is like being born with one leg shorter than the other. This is not a problem that can be solved, but only a condition that must be lived with, by adopting certain remedial changes in shoes and so forth.

The media are inherently sensationalist in their coverage

The first of these structural factors is the nature of the media. This factor is relatively easy to dispose, not because it isn't serious, but because so much has been written about how the requirements of the media cause distortions; the need for simplification, drama, immediacy. Television, the pre-eminent distributor of information, is a visual and personal medium. While not a new observation, this is important to recall in terms of recognizing how risks are covered. People, especially people in pain or afraid, make for dramatic television. The fact that scientific exposition does not make for dramatic television is amply evidenced by the difference in the viewing audiences and success of television 'news magazines' and talkshows compared to science shows.

The creation of factual illusions

The second structural factor is, in some ways, more interesting. This is the manner in which distortions in perceptions are created by the manner in which people process information. To describe this, the notion of a *factual illusion* is convenient. *Optical* illusions are relatively easy to create and actually yield much useful information about how the brain processes visual data. Optical illusions can be created accidentally or deliberately by taking advantage of how the brain takes exceedingly complex, muddled and conflicting information and tries to simplify it in a way that can be readily processed – seen. The study of optical illusions yields useful information about brain function.

Factual illusions occur for precisely the same reasons, and are similarly useful. People process complex and confusing information in ways dictated by training, education and understanding of science and mathematics.

The public is scientifically illiterate and innumerate

The problem of scientific illiteracy and mathematical innumeracy is the subject of much concern. The problem is not isolated to the uneducated. Indeed, the problem is well documented in the well educated. The fact that people do not understand science and mathematics affects how they react to and assimilate information. This applies not only to the general public, but also to members of the media who are conduits of information to the public. Both groups process information differently from experts.

The level of scientific illiteracy is revealed in some apparently trivial but telling results of national polls. About 60 per cent of the American population believe that dinosaurs and people lived at the same time. About half the population does not know that an electron is much smaller than an atom. About one fourth of the population does not know that the earth orbits the sun; half the population does not know how long it takes the earth to go around the sun. This fundamental level of ignorance revealed by polls suggests how ludicrous it is to expect an understanding of the sophisticated concepts that are part of many public health and risk debates. Many scientists and experts have their own anecdotes about the scientific illiteracy they encounter in the general public, and in their dealings with members of the media. Serious errors are made in in strategies to communicate health risks without incorporating a realization of the manner in which people process what they are told.

The problems are equally serious when it comes to statistics and probability. This is often an area of exceptional importance in explaining issues relating to health and medicine and studies relating to them. One survey found, for example, that 43 per cent of those polled believe there is such a thing as a lucky number. (This, in part, explains the appeal of lotteries.) When it comes to statistics and probability, people expect uniformity where lumpiness is the reality. They expect smooth distributions when clusters are normal. Thus when a cluster of a disease occurs, it is never assumed to be a natural phenomenon; rather it is assumed to be caused by some contemporaneous or co-located event. A cluster of miscarriages among pregnant women in one office building sparked a national panic regarding video display terminals. It turns out that the women in the subject building all worked at word processors. They also all wore shoes. The correlation with the miscarriages is specious with both objects. But the former involving a new and mysterious possibility (that of electromagnetic fields) stimulated intense media coverage, national paranoia, and massive research projects. The result of the studies: the problem was a normal (although unfortunate) cluster of miscarriages.

One intriguing study of clusters of diseases was performed in the United Kingdom. The analyst found clusters of a specific cancer in the vicinity of military installations. It turns out that the 'installations' were medieval castles. The author of the study (a statistical expert) had simply searched for a disease that clustered around a selected set of physical locations. Careful selection of time, space and events can create such clustering for all diseases and events.

An interesting study of the problems of perceptions regarding statistical reality was performed by Professor Blackmore at the University of Bristol. The object of the study was to determine if there was a difference in mathematical literacy between those who believed in the paranormal (termed 'sheep' in the study) and those who did not believe in the paranormal (termed 'goats'). Two groups of people were selected based on these criteria – groups with comparable education – and were provided with a short, very simple test on statistics and probability. The results: 'sheep' did very poorly, 'goats' did well evidencing a basic understanding of probability.

What does this mean? One of the questions related to knowing the average probability of the head of a coin turning up in a large number of sets of flips in which a coin was flipped 20 times in each set. The correct answer is 10; the 'goats' got it right. The average answer from the 'sheep' was seven. Thus, one might suppose, if the 'sheep' were involved in or observed an event in which the reality led to something happening ten times – but they believed that the natural occurence for that event was seven times – they would view the reality as strange and be looking for an explanation for the 'increased' incidence in the paranormal, or industrial pollution for example.

This cleavage affects reactions to all data and information. Not to labour the point, but to put it simply in terms of how our brains work; the way in which we process information will affect how we see the world. It affects how we simplify and for those labouring under the limitations of scientific and mathematical illiteracy, factual illusions are created.

How the health activists profit from factual illusions

Understanding how factual illusions are created is where the artistry of health activism comes into play. Knowing how to create these illusions for the news media, and knowing which forum to work in to take advantage of the structural realities of the media becomes an important skill. Just as optical illusions permit one line to look longer than another, even when it is not; activists can deliberately create factual illusions that make one risk look bigger than another. The field of health and risk regulation is scattered with factual mirages. Just as optical illusions are difficult to discern, so too are factual illusions difficult to disassemble. Again, this is not merely because of social and political beliefs, but also because of the way in which people process information.

The challenge for the professional community is to help journalists recognize the components of factual illusions. Just as a measuring instrument, a ruler, can destroy the optical illusion of two identical lines looking different, so too, can 'instruments' – typically in the form of motivated experts – destroy factual illusions.

10 If Claims of Harm from Technology are False, Mostly False, or Unproven, What Does That Tell Us About Science?

Aaron Wildavsky

Introduction

Not a day goes by without charges that products of technology harm the human body and the physical environment. The very earth itself is said to be in serious danger. Hence a series of measures are proposed to avoid or reduce these grave damages. Indeed, without exaggeration, it could be claimed that ours is the environmental age, the time in which technology ceased to be a liberating force and became, instead, a mechanism for self-enslavement, as if the things we created were destroying us.

Viewing with environmental alarm, it is safe to say, has won over public opinion in Western nations. Substantial majorities favour strong and expensive measures to clean up the environment and protect public health. In response, critics of these programs generally complain that environmental regulations are too onerous or too expensive or both. They characterise environmental and safety measures as extreme, suggesting that a more moderate pace and less expensive taste would suit society better.

If the patient is very sick, however, the remedy may have to be severe. If the costs of technological progress are becoming increasingly harmful, then it might well be wise to pay up big now rather than wait until it is too late. With the implications of these assumptions I agree; it is just the 'ifs' I doubt.

The claims of harm from technology, I believe, are false, mostly false, or unproven. To justify this conclusion I will review the relationship between scientific knowledge and governmental action in a broad spectrum of claims about low-level exposure to chemicals. (Studies of global warming, acid rain, and the thinning of the ozone layer would, I think, substantiate this argument but cannot be reported here for lack of space.) Along the way I will touch on associated problems from the violation of standard scientific practices, and the choice of statistical models to the related but different realms of risk management and risk assessment. Always, I will be asking the same questions, albeit in different forms: Are the charges true? To what extent? Is there a small or a big gap between knowledge and action? Why? Though I cannot cover all charges of harm from technology, my net is cast wide enough so that trends in the findings should manifest themselves. The overly-earnest, childlike, perhaps naive question - But is it true? - is worth asking and trying to answer. For in these answers lie clues as to the relationship between knowledge and public policy, and therefore between science and democracy in our time.

Not even a cold may accurately be attributed to Love Canal

Let us begin with Love Canal because it is perhaps the best-publicised of the stories about how careless and possibly criminal disposal of chemical wastes has done significant damage to human life. Perhaps the name itself added poignancy to the story. At one time I sat down and read the articles that constitute the scientific literature on Love Canal. From these I concluded that no significant illness, not even a cold, can properly be laid to living near Love Canal. How could there be? Though there definitely was seepage from the Canal, none of the chemical wastes were detected in tests of water or of air; so unless one is going to posit some new miasma theory, how could there be damage when there is no known mechanism of transmission?

Love Canal hit the media in 1978 with allegations that Hodgkins disease, a debilitating cancer, rectal bleeding, and much more were suffered by residents surrounding Love Canal. The incident went national when the New York State Commissioner of Health issued a report entitled 'Love Canal: Public Health Time-bomb'. This report describes the situation as an 'environmental nightmare', constituting a situation of 'grave and imminent peril'. It turns out that these extreme terms were not based on any evidence whatsoever concerning illness of people surrounding Love Canal but rather, as Marc Landy put it,

...was dictated by legal and fiscal exigencies. In order to obtain funds for health studies, state law required a finding of "grave and imminent peril". Similarly, in order to make Love Canal eligible for federal disaster aid, the health department had to claim that an emergency existed.[1]

By August, Governor Carey of New York announced that all 236 families surrounding the Canal would be permanently relocated, an act that was followed by residents further from the Canal claiming that all sorts of ills were due to the effects of its noxious chemicals.[2]

Two sets of studies of the health hazards at Love Canal were instrumental in raising public apprehension and inciting regulatory action. The first, carried out by Dr Beverly Paigen, a researcher at Roswell Park Memorial Institute in Buffalo in association with volunteers from the Love Canal Homeowners Association, claimed an increase in asthma, urinary disorders, suicides, epilepsy, spontaneous abortions, birth defects, low birth weight babies, slow-growing children, cancer and other grievous conditions.[3] Dr Paigen selected a group of residents who complained about various illnesses and had them fill out questionnaires without seeking medical examinations to determine whether their complaints were medically justified, or using as a control residents of other areas. The second set of studies was commissioned by the EPA in 1980. One of these studies sought to determine whether chromosomal defects (ie genetic damage) existed among the Love Canal residents that could be attributed to the chemical seepage. The other monitored nerve conduction velocities among the residents to see whether there was nervous impairment as a result of living near Love Canal. Then panic hit the streets. Both studies claimed to find evidence of harm, and within four days after these results were made public (well before any scientific review had taken place), President Carter declared an emergency and ordered the evacuation of the remaining 700-odd families, an evacuation that became permanent after a few months.[4]

How have these studies stood up to later review? Concerning the earlier study of Beverly Paigen, a committee of scientists appointed by New York Governor Carey (and headed by Dr Lewis Thomas, chief of the Memorial Sloan-Kettering Cancer Center,

113

and including Dr Arthur Upton, former head of the National Cancer Institute) described it as 'literally impossible to interpret' because of its lack of adequate controls and failure to validate the illnesses claimed. Subsequent studies by the New York State Department of Health also failed to confirm Paigen's claims. Concerning the chromosome study, the Commission found it to be flawed because it too lacked a control group - one matched for current and past medical therapies, work-place chemical exposures, and other factors known to be associated with genetic damage, and whose chromosome samples could be processed simultaneously with those from exposed residents and scored 'blind' (ie without the scorer knowing which were the control and which the exposed samples). None of the scientists who attempted to replicate these results could do so from the slides involved. The final judgement on this study was rendered by the Center for Disease Control in 1983, which undertook a new survey, this one with matched controls and with simultaneous processing and blind scoring. No excess of damaged chromosomes was detected.

Concerning the nerve conduction study, its release had been prematurely forced by leaking to the *New York Times* before any statistical analysis had been performed; once this was carried out, the 'positive' findings that seemed evident on visual inspection vanished.[5]

The latest news is that the houses surrounding Love Canal are being refurbished and new residents are moving in.[6] There is also another outcome. Under the title of 'Awards for Global Environment Crusaders', Lois Marie Gibbs, then a housewife at Love Canal, who became an environmental advocate, was presented with an award of $60,000.[7]

Is Superfund good for our health?

The Superfund program of cleaning up toxic waste sites is a direct response to the appearance of distraught families and plunging property values in the Love Canal episode. From a beginning of about one and a half billion dollars per year it now amounts to over $10 billion. What are we getting for the money? A significant portion goes to lawyers. The General Accounting Office has said there may be over 400,000 such sites. Merely assessing that number would cost more than the $10 billion appropriated for this program.

Another priority problem is the felt necessity of cleaning up every last little bit of the offending chemical because costs escalate as one gets over the 80 or 90 per cent level. The EPA's own study, *Unfinished Business*, concludes that the 'total health impacts [of Superfund sites] do not appear to match public concern in most areas'. Paul Portney gives an example of one of the worst hazard waste sites in Nashua, New Hampshire, where clean-up is estimated to reduce life-time cancer incidence by one every 21 years.[8]

Leo Levenson, then a student at the Graduate School of Public Policy in Berkeley, wrote,

> When I was a Superfund project manager with the US Environmental Protection Agency (EPA) overseeing investigation and clean-up work at toxic waste sites, I became uncomfortable with the suspicion that our clean-up standard for carcinogenic chemicals was so stringent that we spent most of our efforts trying to get rid of tiny, probably harmless quantities of carcinogens.[9]

Levenson goes on to discuss what EPA means by 'cancer-causing'. Over a 70-year constant exposure period to some substance, the EPA sets a standard of one excess cancer in a million, or 10^{-6} cancers. With one out of every four people getting some form of cancer before they die, this would amount to exceeding the quarter million total by one, ie 250,001. Were we to assume that naturally occurring carcinogens produce damage at the same rate, ie 10^{-6}, excess deaths would be as much as 100,000 times greater. 'The fact that *everybody* does not get cancer becomes extraordinary', Levenson concludes, 'unless we assume that the risk extrapolation procedure overestimates low-dose risks from carcinogens'.[10]

Why so expensive? Suppose, to take one of Levenson's examples, the clean-up level for trichloroethylene (TCE), an industrial solvent, is five parts per million when found in water. Very roughly, this is equivalent to getting five drops of water out of an Olympic-sized swimming pool. Should there be a hundred parts per billion of TCE in water, the water could be pumped out and cleaned to only a hundred parts per billion in about a year, though at considerable expense. When that safety standard is dropped to five parts per billion, the clean up could take ten years.[11] Why one

115

in a million? There is no scientific reason. Levenson is probably on the right track when he conjectures that one in a million is commonly conceived to be an exceedingly small probability. 'We say to our loved one', he writes, '"you're one in a million", not, "you're one in a hundred-thousand"'.

Are there no real dangers? That depends on how long an exposure to how much under which conditions.

Confusing risk assessment with risk management: low-level emissions from coke ovens[12]

Consider emissions from coke ovens used in making steel. Experience in the United States, Japan, and Britain shows that coke workers on coke ovens, depending on the degree of their exposure, face risks of early death from respiratory system cancers above those of the general population. The experience of steel workers in Allegheny County, Pennsylvania, demonstrates that relative hazards depend both on years of exposure and where in relation to the ovens - topside being worst, sides being second worst, not being near ovens best - the individual is situated.[13]

The question I am raising has to do with the effects of very low amounts of emissions of coke ovens to which people outside the plants are exposed. These are so low they cannot be directly measured. There is no appropriate mathematical model. This is where so-called 'conservative assumptions' come in. The first important assumption is that there is no threshold level below which exposure does not matter. Instead EPA assumes a constantly increasing linear relationship between any amount of exposure and cancer risks in excess of those suffered by the general population. Such an assumption violates the ascending dose relationships observed among plant workers. The second conservative assumption is that instead of using what is called the maximum likelihood estimator measuring the probability of a finding estimating true risk, they use the upper-bound at the 95 per cent confidence level. This increases the amount of risk over 16 times. The third conservative assumption is that every individual living within 50 kilometres of a coke plant will be exposed every day in the year to the maximum amount, whether indoors or outdoors, in cars closer or further from the plant and regardless of weather conditions. If readers will ask how much time they spend outdoors versus indoors, it would be the unusual person who spent more than half outdoors. A fourth conservative assumption is that individuals do not die from other causes outside coke emissions over the entire 70 years of exposure. Finally, given a choice between models of coke emissions for specific plants, which are more accurate, or models based on assumptions about how the 43 plants in this area would disperse their emissions, which are less accurate, the EPA chose the general models that estimated emissions to be two to four times greater.[14]

Observe that each assumption is biased in favour of finding larger emissions and larger effects. Observe also that some of these conservative assumptions are calculable and others are not. Consequently, the total amount of conservatism in the estimate, ie the bias in favour of much larger effects, is unknown, albeit very large. This confuses risk assessment, which ought to be the best effort to figure out the dangers involved, and risk management, the choice by public authorities of how much risk ought to be taken. By biasing risk estimates in unknown directions many times over, the risk managers are deprived of information on how far they are going in one direction or another.[15] The effect of upward biases is to increase the cost per cancer avoided from EPA's figure of $6.8 million to $682 million. As a bonus we also get to see a rise in the Benzene cost from $58.8 million per early deaths estimated to be avoided, itself a very large number, to $5,880 million.[16]

Now that the process of upward biasing has been illustrated, we are in a position to better understand how the evacuation of Times Beach, Missouri, was justified. Entering this study as amateurs, we should develop our 'street smarts' in Times Beach.

Panic without purpose: Times Beach, Missouri

Just as the residents of Times Beach, Missouri, a town around 25 miles west of St Louis, were astonished to see EPA officials dressed in moon suits (gloves, plastic suits, respirators) picking up soil samples from the streets, citizens of the United States (myself included) were astonished at the forced evacuation of this little town on grounds its soil had been subject to fatal contamination. The culprit was dioxin, which had been used as part of waste oil to spray roads in the early 1970s. Dioxin had gained its fame as the most (or one of the most) deadly poisons known to mankind because tiny amounts kill some laboratory animals such as guinea pigs. The other side of the story is that amounts thousands of times greater are required to knock off hamsters. And while very large amounts cause cancers in rats and mice, a huge explosion of dioxin in Seveso, Italy, caused a considerable amount of chloracne but not a single death among humans.[17]

EPA assumed that people would not stick to roads and paths or avoid contaminated places but rather that all damage would be equally felt everywhere. Thus amounts of dioxin in street dust and house dust were rendered equivalent. By multiplying one extreme safety factor times another, a final criterion of a part per billion units of dioxin was established as a safe level. The trouble is that almost anything can be found at that level. It implies that the human organism is so sensitive that the least little thing would set it off in destructive decline. Faced with the impossible task of preventing such a phenomenon from occurring, EPA decided it was cheaper to pay $33 million to buy out the whole town and have it abandoned.

If substantial exposures to dioxin on the part of industrial workers do not show ill effects over many years, why should trace amounts in the soil do so in Missouri? There was no evidence of elevated amounts of dioxin in bodies of Times Beach residents. Of course, there were undoubtedly people in Times Beach and everywhere else who have health problems, but that is another matter. Times Beach is a case of panic without purpose. The Agent Orange affair has a purpose but not a persuasive rationale.

Agent Orange

During the Vietnam War airforce planes sprayed between 10 and 12 million gallons of a herbicide called Agent Orange (active agent, dioxin) as a defoliant. In the 1970s a group of veterans brought a suit against the manufacturers of Agent Orange, after which thousands of veterans asked for compensation for damages. Now everyone in the United States and perhaps even the world is exposed to dioxin because it is a by-product of other processes, including the burning of wood, gasoline, and municipal wastes. The background levels of Americans who have had no direct contact with dioxin or Agent Orange ranges from two to 20 parts per trillion. Those Vietnam veterans who served in the most likely places to have been exposed and non-Vietnam veterans are well within that range at five parts per trillion. In epidemiological studies, the Centers for Disease Control discovered that certain Vietnam War veterans were likely to develop non-Hodgkin's lymphoma but that the highest occurrence came from Navy veterans who served on ships many miles off-shore where no whiff of Agent Orange was possible. (The Veterans Administration authorised payments to the sailors because they had trouble not because their trouble had anything to do with Agent Orange.) Other studies were done on the 1,038 airforce personnel who loaded Agent Orange on planes and threw it out as compared to 19,101 airforce veterans who were not exposed at all. The handlers, like the men who patrolled areas where Agent Orange was used, did have larger amounts of dioxin in their bodies but no difference in illnesses. As each claim is refuted, new ones are made, such as the allegation that this or that group was actually exposed the most. The basic support comes from a number of Swedish studies that identify what are called soft-tissue sarcomas with minor exposure to dioxin. These results have not been replicated in any other studies. The people studied had been exposed only for a few days. Why then were factory workers involved in the production of dioxin, exposed to incomparably greater amounts, not harmed in this way?[18]

The Alar Hoax

In the 1960s the Uniroyal Corporation tested a growth retardant on apple trees that kept the apples firmer and redder and on the trees longer. The chemical used was called daminozide. After company tests suggested no health risks, it was marketed under the name Alar. A decade later a researcher at the University of Nebraska Medical Center, Bella Toth, gave huge amounts of Alar to various kinds of rodents and discovered that they developed tumours. Uniroyal claimed the study was invalid because the amount of Alar fed to these rodents exceeded the maximum tolerated dose (MTD) animals are expected to withstand. Other studies suggested that by-products of Alar were increased during food processing. EPA began studying the growth retardant and in 1985 banned Alar. Uniroyal appealed to EPA's Scientific Advisory Panel composed of

119

scientists nominated by the National Science Foundation and the National Institutes of Health. Essentially the committee decided that, because of numerous flaws, poor record-keeping, lack of concurrent control groups, and the massive doses, the tests were not useful for predicting human risks. EPA delayed its ban and ordered more tests to see if Alar caused genetic damage. It didn't. EPA kept insisting that the MTD fed to the same animals be increased once, twice and then four times until eventually tumours appeared. The ban was imposed.[19]

In the meantime, the Natural Resources Defense Council (NRDC) and Ralph Nader, consumer advocate, got together with others to ask that Alar be banned right away. Calling Alar a carcinogen, they pressed their case in newspapers and began calling and writing to large grocery chains and food processors to stop purchasing food treated with Alar. They came close to their goal but did not quite reach it and NRDC decided to take a different route.[20] NRDC chose Robin Whyatt, who had a MA in public health, and Janet Hathaway, who had degrees in law and philosophy, to do a report on Alar. They also chose two other scientists to review the work calling it a peer review committee. (Peer review, of course, means the work is reviewed independently by scientists chosen by journals or established bodies.) At the same time, NRDC hired David Fenton, a public relations consultant to create a campaign to get its message across. The thrust was to be that Alar harmed children. The medium was to be the '60 Minutes' program watched by millions of people. A news conference was scheduled the very next day together with appearances on talk shows and major magazine articles. The report was kept from other media in order to give '60 Minutes' priority and to maintain surprise and therefore impact.[21]

Waving the NRDC report, 'Intolerable Risk: Pesticides In Our Children's Food', showing a skull and crossbones to make sure viewers got the point, '60 Minutes' presenter Ed Bradley termed Alar 'The most potent cancer-causing agent in our food supply', echoing the NRDC claim that some 5,300 children might well get cancer by ingesting UDMH, a by-product that occurred when fruit with Alar on it was converted into juice or apple sauce. The headline in *USA Today* was typical: 'Fear: Are We Poisoning Our Children?'.

Actress Meryl Streep organised 'Mothers and Others for Pesticide Limits', while anxious mothers threw apple juice and apple sauce down the drain and apple sales dropped precipitously.

The British Government's Advisory Committee on Pesticides concluded that 'Even for children consuming the maximum quantities of apples and apple juice, subjected to the maximum treatment with daminozide, there is no risk'. Motivated by the widespread concern over the effects of Alar, 14 scientific societies, composed of toxicologists, nutritionists, and food scientists, issued a joint report stating that by far the greatest hazard in the food supply came not from pesticides but from naturally occurring toxins and bacteria. The director of the Food and Drug Administration's Office of Toxicological Sciences, Robert Scheuplein, stated in unmistakable terms that the food supply was safe, that in regard to risk of cancer barely one-tenth of one per cent could be attributed to pesticides coming from industry.[22]

What arguments lay behind the claims that the objections to Alar were misguided? One was that an Alar-tainted apple, if it were carcinogenic at all, would have about a third to a half of the carcinogenic potency of a glass of Berkeley tap water, such water containing chlorine, which creates chloroform, which is a very weak carcinogen. Another was that to get a human dose equivalent to that fed to the rats a human being would need to drink something like 19,000 bottles of apple juice.

In a long letter to *Science*, biochemist Bruce Ames and his collaborator, statistician Lois Gold, observed that all plants produce poisons to protect themselves against predators; the result is that nature's own pesticides outrank synthetic pesticides produced by industry over 10,000 to 1 by weight and potency per day. Nor do the various human defences against these poisons distinguish whether they are dealing with natural or manmade substances. It is not merely Alar they reasoned, but all pesticides put together as they enter the food chain whose effects are minimal. (Who would know, to take a different but related example, that during the Chilean grape scare, where two grapes had three micrograms each of cyanide, that a lima bean, untouched by synthetic pesticides, contains over a hundred micrograms without doing anyone harm?) Gold and Ames estimated from a comparison of the poisonous potential of virtually every substance ever tested on animals that the possible carcinogenic potential of UDMH as it broke down from Alar during processing (if one drank a six-ounce glass of apple juice a day during a lifetime of 70 years) was 0.0017, less than the poisonous content of a single mushroom or of the alcohol consumed in one's daily glass of orange juice. And then there were the over a hundred other chemicals in apple juice that have not yet been tested. Moreover, they argued there was damage to health in banning Alar because apples would fall to the ground earlier and be at greater risk of entry by insects, which would require more insecticides. Untreated apples, moreover, would be likely to have more mold toxins, substances considerably more dangerous than Alar or UDMH.[23]

Alar is still banned, consumer confidence has been shaken, apple growers have been harmed, all without either basic reasons in the science of the subject to believe the product was harmful or experimental evidence to that effect. Given that there are a number of studies, only those which accord with others and which are conducted according to commonly recognised criteria of excellence, with appropriate controls, impersonal assessment, and peer review deserve credence.[24] Yet on that basis there is no discernible damage.

Even at two per cent of the diet of experimental animals, a level at which table salt would be severely toxic, Alar is not a carcinogen.[25] Upon processing, Alar breaks down to UDMH. Yet mice fed between 10 and 20 parts per million of UDMH showed no effect although this dose was 22,000 times higher than NRDC claimed children ingested. By the time the mice were fed between 40 and 80 parts per million, their tumours were, as C F Chaisson said, 'merely a consequence of severe liver toxicity'. She continues that 'since daminozide and UDMH do not cause genetic damage, an argument that exposure to low levels of these chemicals early in life would cause tumours later in life has no credibility'.[26] This line of reasoning is important because it goes to the heart of what is considered cancerous. The major criterion used to be damage to DNA, ie genetic damage. If this criterion is followed (as distinguished from ability to cause tumours at the MTD), most claims of carcinogenicity based on animal tests would fail.

When all we've got isn't good enough: low-level rodent carcinogens fail as human predictors

The basic idea behind regulation has been to protect workers, consumers, and the public at large from exposure to cancer-causing chemicals, be it saccharin, nitrate, cyclamate, formaldehyde (in the form of home insulation), asbestos, PCBs, dioxins, or whatever. But this presupposes that there is a means of identifying which chemicals are carcinogenic and of estimating the degree of damage they pose to humans. The chief method now in use is high dose animal (usually rats or mice) cancer tests. The supposition has been that such tests are valid. Scepticism expressed by a few scientists to the effect that cancers might be induced only at (and indeed, largely as a consequence of) the extremely high doses fed to animals, the amount just below what would kill, have been dismissed until recently. After all it would be horrendously expensive to test at low doses when tumours might not show up for years.

In 'Too Many Rodent Carcinogens: Mitogenesis Increases Mutagenesis', Ames and Gold conclude that cell division (mitogenesis) increases susceptibility to cancer (mutagenesis). This leads them to conclude that the low exposures to which most human beings are usually exposed may have little or no effect in promoting cancer '...and often will be zero. Thus, without studies of the mechanism of carcinogenesis, the fact that a chemical is a carcinogen at the MTD in rodents provides no information about low-dose risk to humans'. This is a direct frontal assault on the entire theory that high-dose exposures to rodents can tell us anything.[27]

In sum, then, newer evidence is bringing into serious doubt the basis for identifying carcinogens that underlies priority setting and decision making in government. Investment decisions, insurance payments, legal fees, liability awards, and pollution control costs mounting into many billions of dollars have been determined by such tests; yet the scientific basis for such decisions is exceedingly shaky. I believe a much stronger verdict is called for. Rodent tests are bound to be misleading. The science is weak. Even if it were stronger, however, it would be misleading to rely on them because the indispensable statistical procedures for going from animals to people are fatally flawed. Why? Statistical models cannot overcome woefully inadequate knowledge.

No statistical model is appropriate, yet choice of model determines outcomes

In doing the double extrapolation from high doses to effects at low doses and simultaneously from rodents (or other animals) to humans, there is no way to choose among the available statistical models, which give widely varying results. Let me state as forcefully as I can the implication of this rather antiseptic sentence: choice of model will determine whether there is some connection or no connection to cancer or whether the connection is slim or strong. If we asked directions and were told that there are a variety of models available for calculation that will take us in opposite directions without there being any reason to prefer one over the other, we would be in the same position as those assessing cancer risks to humans from rodent data.

In the usual experimental protocol, some rodents get the MTD and two other sets get different fractions and a third, the control group, none at all. There also have to be two sexes. This creates twelve groups of animals; conventionally and for cost reasons studies start with fifty each. Given that human doses vary from ten to a thousand and more times less than that given to rodents, the question arises as to whether there is a dose response model in which one can have confidence. This is not a call for perfection, as if to say that all models are lacking in some respect so all are equally (in)valid. As David Freedman and Hans Zeisel say in their seminal paper,

> Dose response models are imperfect. Nor was the maiden voyage of the Titanic a great success. Such understatements conceal more than they reveal. There are degrees of imperfection in theories ranging from quantum mechanics to astrology.[28]

The one-hit model (even a molecule of the offending substance can cause cancer), it turns out, does not fit data from most animal experiments. Various multi-hit and multi-stage models, essentially Markov chain equations in which the future is dependent on successive stages of the past, however, fit the data all too well. The trouble is that these models cannot be distinguished on the basis of adequacy. In addition they require strict assumptions that are extremely unlikely to be met in what we might call the real world of the human body: that the cancer causing process proceeds through each and every stage in fixed and irreversible sequence; that the times in between stages are independent of each other and follow the exponential, Poisson distribution, assuming also that exposure is constant; that competing hazards (after all, mice and people can and do die of other things) are independent of one another; and that cells, which are the target of this enterprise, also go through the stages independently of each other. A table Freedman and Zeisel provide (see *Table 1*) shows that among five well-known chemical substances that have been objects of attention, the different models vary hundreds of thousands of times over. Where saccharin is concerned, the published estimates vary over five million times. What could be more damning to the entire enterprise than their conclusion:

> To sum up, the choice of models has a decisive impact on low-dose risk estimates, and in the present state of knowledge there is no sound way to pick one model rather than another. All except the one-hit will fit typical dose-response data sets, and none have adequate biological foundations. That is why reliable estimates of risks at low dose cannot be made on the basis of present knowledge.[29]

Table 1: The impact of the model on low-dose risk estimates

Substance	one-hit	multi-stage	Weibull	multi-hit
Aflatoxin	1	30	1,000	40,000
Dioxin	1	400	400	800
DMNA	1	700	700	2,700
Dieldrin	1	3	200	1,000
DDT	1	2	70	200

Source: Freedman and Zeisel, p.21

The man-to-mouse (or rat) problem is equally as daunting as going from high to low doses. Rats and mice do not extrapolate well to each other. In a major study by Haseman et al in 1984, of the 88 compounds tested, 43 were carcinogenic in at least one of the two test species, '17 were positive in mice and rats both. 14 were positive in mice only (and) 12 were positive in rats only'.[30] Then, again, when six 'model rodent carcinogens', were tested on monkeys, which are supposed to be, according to evolutionists, a lot closer to human beings, five out of six were negative. Often it is said in rebuttal that all human carcinogens are also animal carcinogens. Aside from confusing conditional probabilities, so that even if most human carcinogens were animal carcinogens the reverse would not follow, the statement is untrue. Our best knowledge is that the 'if human, then animal' proposition is true in 59 percent but therefore untrue in 41 percent of the instances examined.[31] This is better than chance but not much.

Aware of the oft-raised question of how to regulate carcinogens if animal tests will not do, Freedman and Zeisel nevertheless conclude that 'it may be advisable to give up the pretence of a scientific foundation where none exists'. Study the basic science and learn more is their recommendation. But '...obscuring the scientific uncertainties cannot be good public policy'. I agree. A Ouija board lacks the patina of science but it would do as well (or badly) as rodent tests.[32]

How much cancer are we talking about?

Further perspective on regulation of cancer risk may be had by following biologist Michael Gough in his estimation of the amount of cancer EPA can regulate. Assuming that EPA is accurate in its risk estimations, if complete control were established over all carcinogens it is allowed to regulate, around 1.3 percent of the present approximately 485,000 annual deaths due to cancer would be prevented. Were the Food and Drug Administration's (FDA) methods of estimation used (FDA uses relative body weights to scale small animals to humans while EPA proceeds by comparing relative surface areas), preventable excess cancers would go from 6400 attributable to the EPA method to 1400 (a quarter of one per cent total cancer deaths).[33] A great part of the deaths associated from indoor air pollution are associated with cigarette smoking, which EPA cannot prevent. When tobacco-caused cancers are eliminated from the total, the amount of excess deaths attributable to EPA regulations goes way down to anywhere from 124 to 1240. Thus it turns out that those kinds of cancers that depend on personal behaviour and are not easily subject to any sort of regulation amount to about half of the number EPA regulations might prevent. Not surprisingly, Gough concludes '...that despite the agency's best efforts, there will be little impact on cancer rates'.[34]

Decreasing health in the name of safety: the rise and fall of Bovine Growth Hormone (Somatotropin)

Why does it matter that charges of human and environmental damage from technology are entirely or largely untrue? The short answer is that people will not be able to take advantage of technology that improves health, and that unnecessary expenditure will make them, and hence their physical environment, poorer than need be. The travail of the bovine growth hormone and the ripping out of asbestos from school rooms tell this story.

In the past the development of a new technology that would drastically reduce the cost of producing milk by a quarter to a half and promised to do even more, so that in the words of a Cornell group, '...the rate of productivity change [would rise] above any level previously experienced in the human attempt to harness biological systems for mankind's benefit',[35] would have been greeted with acclaim. What could be better for society, especially for the nation's and the world's poorest people than to have this exceptionally nutritious food made much more affordable. Not in our time. Instead, active effort has been made to keep BST from the market with accusations ranging from unnatural to unsafe to adding to the world's milk surpluses. As Bill Richards reported in *The Wall Street Journal*, under the headline 'Sour Reception Greets Milk Hormone', scientific evidence stated that this product of genetic engineering was entirely safe and the FDA was expected to approve it (which it has) 'but it may already be too late'. Although milk made with BST can in no way be distinguished from milk without it, most supermarket chains said they would not handle it because, as a spokesman for Safeway said, 'we don't want our customers or stores being used as guinea pigs'. Studies show that the mere mention of the word 'hormone' or 'additive' puts people off. A marketing consultant for Dairy Queen reported watching a TV program in which consumers showed 'instant sympathy against the drug companies and for the critics'. 'This is a market associated with small children', the man from Kraft USA said. 'It's very sensitive. We're going to follow our consumers' concerns on this'.[36] Well, this is consumer sovereignty of a sort. The most poignant comment came from a manager for American Cyanamid who stated wistfully that 'we have to rely on science and the FDA to ultimately win the day'.[37] Pity the poor protagonist reduced to relying on the truth!

Produced by animals' pituitary glands, growth hormones are 'species specific' in that each type of cow produces its own. Cows themselves produce minute quantities of BST, a fact that has been known for a half century. Until recently, however, the cost has been prohibitive in that it would require BST from the glands of some 200 cows to provide a single daily dose. Biotechnology now makes mass production at low cost possible.

On April 1, 1986, an appropriate day, the Foundation on Economic Trends, led by Jeremy Rifkin, the Humane Society of the United States, the Wisconsin Family Farm Defense Fund, and the Secretary of State of Wisconsin asked FDA to conduct an environmental impact statement on BST, an unusual request that was quickly rejected. The petitioners argued that the 'internal environment' of cows will be made worse by lameness, udder infection, fatty livers, and other diseases. They also believe that there will be a requirement for special feed stocks that will alter patterns of land use and that dairy surpluses will hurt small farmers.[38] Tests in Europe and the United States demonstrate considerable increase in milk yields without deleterious effects on animals or on humans.[39] A report in *Science* on the FDA study concludes 'that the use of recombinant bovine growth hormone (rbGH) [the technical name for BST] in dairy cattle presents no increased health risk to consumers. Bovine GH is not biologically active in humans...'[40]

An article by two FDA researchers covers not only the FDA's work but 30 years of studies. 'We'd like to get our side of the story out, to show why we're comfortable with the safety. We'd like for people to know that it's a thoughtful process, and we want it to be open and credible.'[41] Gibbons notes that Samuel S Epstein, a professor of occupational and environmental medicine at the University of Illinois College of Medicine, known for his work claiming there was an epidemic of cancer in the United States, 'published a paper in the little known (and non-peer-reviewed) *International Journal of Health Services* charging that the FDA had abdicated its regulatory responsibility by relying on research done by industry and industry's "indentured academics"'.

Co-author of the FDA paper, C Greg Guyer, replied that 'Everyone in the whole science world except for Dr Epstein would not think [rbGH] ever would be active in humans'. Even when the hormone was injected intravenously into children suffering from dwarfism, it was not active. 'Yet', Gibbons continues, 'Epstein's report has had consequences. It caused four grocery chains and several food-processing companies to refuse milk from treated herds...'.

There are products, unlike BST, that are dangerous at some level. If the product is essential, however, the relevant question is the comparative one, compared to what will take its place. Often, this essential question is neither asked nor answered.

Hazel, how's your husband? Compared to whom? EDB? Compared to what?

There is to begin with, no doubt whatsoever that ethylene dio-bromide (EDB) at some dose does cause cancer in laboratory animals. It is widely used as a grain fumigant and should be handled with care. Nevertheless, unless there is a better alternative, this does not at all mean that EDB should be banned or that the trace amounts that end up in various foods, such as cake mixes, constitute any danger whatsoever to those who ingest them. EPA estimated that individuals consume approximately five to ten micrograms of EDB a day. It did not say, because that would have ruined its case at the outset, that each of us typically takes in some 140,000 micrograms of pepper per day. Five to ten micrograms are approximately one-quarter millionth of what rats were given considering the ratio between our and their body weights. Two or three extra cases of cancer per thousand, EPA estimated, would be caused over a lifetime by exposure to these tiny amounts of EDB. This is a one per cent increase over a lifetime, not trivial but not large. In fact it is too small to be detected by means of the usual epidemiological studies in human beings. What happens, we might ask, when human beings are exposed to amounts of EDB five to ten thousand times greater than the average individual for 16 years? Three such studies have been conducted and from them we can conclude that EPA vastly exaggerates the risk. Another bit of evidence is that in California, after extensive hearings, 130 parts per billion, ten times larger than the amount EPA thought was safe, was considered sufficient to protect workers in a lifetime of exposure. The industrial exposure limit is 10 milligrams per worker per day, a thousand times larger than the EPA margin. It is also easy to show that pepper and any number of other foods, not only the usual peanut butter example but milk as well, are more dangerous on the EPA basis than EDB.[42]

My main purpose in giving this example, however, is not the usual one of demonstrating exaggeration but of considering alternatives. Even if EDB was as dangerous as EPA stated, grain and grain products are essential to the food supply, so there had to be an alternative that was better in the sense of some combination of safer and no more expensive before it should be subject to ban. Expense comes in because raising the cost reduces the amount purchased.

EDB has marvellous properties heretofore unmentioned. It stinks to high heaven; that is a wonderful quality because it tells workers (who are far more exposed than the ordinary citizen) when EDB is around so they can get out of the way. EDB clings to milling machinery; that is also desirable for worker protection because the alternative is to fumigate entire factories, which would give them much higher doses. EDB is not subject to explosion, a handy quality to have around grain, which kills people now and again from explosions in grain elevators and such places. With the other known alternatives not tested for cancer, with one alternative, irradiation, subject to unwarranted phobias, in my opinion the decision was unwise.

Several months later an article in the *Des Moines Register* tells the story:

> The US Environmental Protection Agency, which last week issued mandatory limits on the use of EDB in grain-based foods, has quietly slashed its assessment of the health risks posed by the chemical.
>
> Richard Johnson, EDB review team leader for the

EPA, said the agency has known for almost three months that its earlier estimate that the widely used grain fumigant could be expected to cause three cases of cancer per 1,000 persons was far too high.

But he said EPA has been under such strong pressure to ban EDB (ethylene dibromide) that no public announcement of its health findings has been issued.[43]

As Dr Sorell L Schwartz, professor of pharmacology at Georgetown University's School of Medicine wrote in a letter about EDB,

A most important and disconcerting observation is that the data on which all of the EDB risk estimates were based are unsuitable for estimation methods the EPA used and the conclusions it reached.

In the study on which the EPA decision was based, EDB was administered to the rat through a tube directly into the stomach, a process known as 'gavage'. Approximately half of the tumours ascribed to EDB were localised in the forestomach, which was exposed to high concentrations of EDB. EDB is an irritant and causes cell death and damage at high concentrations. Current concepts of chemical carcinogenesis suggest that high local tissue levels of such irritants disproportionally increase the incidence of tumours at the site of administration and argue against such tumours being used as the basis for extrapolation of risk to likely levels of exposure from dietary intake.

Another serious fault with the EDB gavage study was that, because of acute toxicity problems, it was necessary to interrupt the dosing of the animals and then continue the dosing at a later time. EPA attempted to correct for this interruption by using a computational method that treated the study as if there had been no interruption. Such an adjustment is unsatisfactory and mathematically increases the potency of the substance tested. Similarly, the risk estimation method involved a modification which had not been peer reviewed by the risk assessment community and which at this date has not been accepted.[44]

131

In whose interest is it for government to give in to hysteria?

Two asbestos tragedies, one based on too little concern, the other on too much

On June 12, 1990, William K Reilly, the Administrator of the Environmental Protection Agency, gave a talk at the American Enterprise Institute on 'Asbestos, Sound Science, and Public Perceptions: Why We Need a New Approach to Risk'. He recalled a conversation upon his appointment with Senator Daniel P Moynihan who said 'Above all - do not allow your agency to become transported by middle-class enthusiasm!' What Moynihan meant, Reilly told his audience, was 'Respect sound science; don't be swayed by the passions of the moment'. As a conservationist, he continued, he had experience with 'the law of unintended consequences'. Asbestos, the miracle fibre, for instance, that would not rust or corrode or burn and has many desirable qualities, was discovered, at high levels of continuous exposure, to cause serious and sometimes fatal diseases from lung cancer to mesothelioma to asbestosis.[45] As the consequences became clearer, EPA and the Occupational Health and Safety Administration (OHSA) drafted regulations to limit the exposure of asbestos workers and the general public. In addition, in 1985 Congress passed legislation mandating inspection and control of asbestos in schools in order to protect children and custodial workers from exposure to asbestos fibres. Now, Reilly paused, after meetings with school officials including a delegation from the United States Catholic Conference and severe criticism of EPA in the media, it became clear to him 'that a considerable gap has opened up between what EPA had been trying to say about asbestos, and what the public has been *hearing* [emphasis in the original]'. He claimed that EPA had been trying to tell the public that it was desirable to manage asbestos in place by covering it up rather than ripping it out of buildings. Instead, school districts began wholesale programs of tearing asbestos out, thereby causing many more fibres to be exposed in the air and possibly harming custodial workers and school children more than leaving the stuff there. Though perhaps others were also to blame, Reilly thought EPA deserved its share for not stating clearly enough what the danger was and how it should be dealt with. So he was commission ing a major management review of EPA communications.

Earlier in his speech, Reilly noted that:

> Most recently, the unusually compelling medical evi-
> dence on asbestos led to my decision last year to phase
> out virtually all *remaining* [emphasis in original] uses of
> asbestos in consumer products, in order to prevent the in-
> troduction of additional asbestos into the environment.

Why? If it was continuous exposure to high levels of asbestos
that led to disease, why would sporadic exposure to comparatively
small amounts necessarily do the same? If small amounts of asbestos could be safely left on pipes and walls and ceilings and all sorts
of other places in schools and buildings, why had there been a total
ban of asbestos products? Now my reading of prior EPA regulations is different from Reilly's in that I think school districts could
reasonably have concluded that they must rid themselves of asbestos, especially since the calculations they were urged to make generally indicated that sort of action. The matter is debatable. Enlightenment is to be had, I think, by focusing on what Reilly left
out.

No doubt Reilly was concerned about the type of headline he
was getting such as 'Risk of One Type of Asbestos Discounted,
Health Experts Say Billions May Be Wasted by Removing Banned
Insulation Material'. What is this about different types of asbestos?
Some scientists claim that the type of fibres present in most school
buildings are safe at non-occupational levels. EPA officials were
quoted as replying that there were '"some studies that give a hint
that some of these fibre types are less likely to cause cancer", but
that given scientific uncertainties "we treat them as of equal
concern"'.[46] Thereby hangs a tale.

Blue asbestos (crocidolite) comes from South Africa and is
deadly; about three months occupational exposure is sometimes
enough to kill. Blue asbestos amounts to about two per cent of the
amount used in the United States. Brown asbestos (amosite),
which accounts for about three per cent of asbestos and also comes
from South Africa, is not user-friendly and has to be handled with
great care if handled at all. These two, brown and blue, are classified as amphibole minerals. In the United States, chrysotile
(which I shall hereafter refer to as white asbestos) is a naturally

occurring mineral. Their shapes differ in that chrysotile is bushy, its fibres congregate together but are easily separable, whereas the two others, the amphibole minerals, are long, pointed and brittle. The crucial difference is that amphiboles are easily absorbed into the lungs and stay there while the chrysotiles being more flexible can break down more easily and are often expelled.

All of us, regardless of race, creed, colour, or environmental position, ingest something like a million to two million fibres a year whether we want to or not. Once one knows that asbestos is naturally found everywhere - air, water, food - the task of ridding ourselves of low-level exposures is seen for what it is, namely, quixotic and counterproductive.

Epidemiologists Sir Richard Doll of Oxford and Professor Julian Peto of the University of London concluded that low-level exposures increase the risk of dying of cancer by 'approximately one death a year' in the whole of the British Isles - too small a number to be considered. (The danger of playing high school football is ten per million.) Dr Hans Weill and Janet Hughes of Tulane University estimated the upper level of deaths from low-level asbestos exposure to be one-quarter of one death per million people. The World Health Organisation study in 1986, 'Asbestos and Other Natural Mineral Fibres', disposes of the matter by saying that 'In the general population, the risks of mesothelioma and lung cancer attributable to asbestos cannot be quantified reliably and are probably undetectably low'. Similarly, in 1984 the 'Report of the Royal Commission on Matters of Health and Safety Arising from the Use of Asbestos in Ontario' states that: 'Even a building whose air has a fibre level up to 10 times greater than that found in typical outdoor air would create a risk of fatality that was less than one-fiftieth the risk of having a fatal automobile accident while driving to and from the building. [Furthermore]...asbestos in building air will almost never pose a health hazard to building occupants'.[47] Nevertheless, legitimised by EPA and promoted by the Sierra Club, The Audobon Society, the Service Employees International Union, and the National Education Association, none of this dissuaded *People Magazine* from headlining: 'Discovering that their home is walled with asbestos, Florida family flees the dangerous dust', or that 'More disturbing than the loss of a home is the prospect of a future tainted with doubt'. *USA Today* is no better: 'There's a killer in the corridors, gyms, or boiler rooms of 40,000 schools across the USA', though it cannot compete with *Good Housekeeping's* heroic 'I saved my family from asbestos contamination'.[48]

Long before a few scientists came forward with views dissenting from the EPA and media consensus there was ample evidence that whereas amphibole asbestos in large amounts was exceedingly dangerous, even causing illnesses in the families of miners so afflicted, white asbestos did very little if any damage to families of workers; indeed, as researchers expressed it in the June 28, 1989, *New England Journal of Medicine*, '...it remains uncertain whether any type of asbestos acting alone can cause lung cancer in non-smokers'. They concluded that:

> In the absence of epidemiological data or estimations of risk that indicate that the health risk of environmental exposure to asbestos are large enough to justify high expenditure of public funds, one must question the unprecedented expense of the order of $100 billion to $150 billion that could result from asbestos abatement.[49]

Evidently concerned about the growing and counterproductive costs of asbestos abatement in schools (then running annually at $4 to $5 billion a year), Brooke (BT) Mossman of the Department of Pathology at the University of Vermont, J Bignon, of INSERM de Recherche sur la Biopathologie et la Tocologie Pulmonaire et Renale, Creteil, France; M Corn, Division of Environmental Health Engineering, School of Hygiene and Public Health, Johns Hopkins University, A Seaton, Institute of Occupational Medicine in Edinburgh, Scotland, and JBL Gee, Director, Winchester Chest Clinic and Professor, Department of Internal Medicine, Yale University School of Medicine (referred to as Mossman and Gee) wrote a review of the literature in the January 19, 1990 *Science* in which they concluded that:

> The available data and comparative risk assessments...indicate that chrysotile asbestos, the type of fibre found predominantly in US schools and buildings is not a health risk in the non-occupational environment. Clearly, the asbestos panic in the US must be curtailed, especially because unwarranted and poorly controlled

135

asbestos abatement results in unnecessary risks to young removal workers who may develop asbestos-related cancers in later decades. The extensive removal of asbestos has occurred less frequently in Europe.[50]

Does one go with preponderant evidence, which favours Mossman et al, or does one ask for proof positive that no damage can ever occur from white asbestos? On that basis, essentially the view that there is no threshold so that even a single fibre can kill a person, virtually nothing could be said to be safe.[51] (On that basis, sufferers from AIDS, as if they did not have enough trouble already, would have to be quarantined on the grounds of residual uncertainty that casual contact might conceivably result in catching this deadly disease.) This led to an editorial in *Science* damning existing practice and thus indirectly the speech by EPA Director Reilly with which we began.[52]

Mesothelioma, which takes some 30 years to develop, is a particularly nasty tumour that crushes the lung and kills the afflicted. It is relatively rare but it does occur. The trouble is that these tumours are difficult to diagnose so one is not sure whether they are under- or over-reported and the tumours occur both in people exposed to different types of asbestos and in the general population, albeit, again, at very low rates. There is evidence from Canada that chrysotile fibres alone, without strong support from other types of asbestos, are unlikely to cause mesotheliomas.[53]

After citing various studies, Mossman et al noted with some asperity that:

> ...fibre concentrations from recent studies in buildings [in the United States, France, and Britain] are comparable to levels in outdoor air, a point surely relevant to assessing the health risk of asbestos in buildings.[54]

Why remove a mineral from buildings that is present in equal concentration in the outside air?

EPA officials did indeed have reason, if not sufficient reason, to think that white asbestos might be sufficiently dangerous to ban or to require removal. As with many other things, the history is essential. In the 1930s and 1940s Dr Irving Selikoff conducted a series of researches into occupational exposure to asbestos and discovered or confirmed, however you take it, that under these conditions various types of asbestos caused serious, even deadly, lung diseases. He was attacked by the industry and he held his ground. As evidence mounted, Selikoff became respected for his research and admired for his integrity. In recent years, while some other researchers differentiated white from brown and blue-green types of asbestos, Selikoff, whose suspicion of the asbestos industry had been honed to a fine point by personal experience, denied it all. Any amount of any colour might well cause grave damage. And he buttressed his claims with new research.[55] In doing this research, Selikoff stuck to his original models in which x-rays were taken of people exposed in various ways to asbestos. While x-rays are good for many purposes, they are not useful in distinguishing types of fibres. For that purpose, only autopsies will do.

Thus we have not only the world's most pre-eminent asbestos researcher insisting there is deadly danger from all types of asbestos in any amount but a difference in research procedures that is hard to adjudicate. Looking at the evidence as a whole as various other researchers have done, distinction among types of and exposures to asbestos seems sensible and from that follows the conclusion that ripping out white asbestos from buildings is counterproductive. Worrying whether Selikoff might not be right again, worrying more that his accusations, bolstered by his hard-won acquaintance with media techniques, would subject those who incurred his wrath to condemnation, EPA decided to play it safe. Whether by playing it safe from attacks on its reputation as insufficiently concerned with citizen welfare, it also became insufficiently concerned with preponderant evidence on this subject, is the question at issue.

In earlier decades, indications of asbestosis were disregarded as workers began to come down with serious ailments. Do we make up for that grievous fault by taking white asbestos away from places and people it does not harm?

In an interview in *Discover* magazine, Steven Schneider, more forthcoming than most, stated that:

>...Scientists should consider stretching the truth to get some broad base support, to capture the public's imagination. That, of course, entails getting loads of media coverage. So we have to offer up scary scenarios, make

simplified, dramatic statements, and make little mention about any doubts we might have…. Each of us has to decide what the right balance is between being effective and being honest.[56]

If everyone is trying to counter someone else's outrageous comments, it will not be possible to figure out even approximately where the truth, insofar as it is known, lies. (I am reminded of the difficulty the Soviet government has had in reconstructing economic, health, and budgetary figures because various people in the past altered them for political purposes without standardizing these alterations.) Righting environmental wrongs, if that is the motivation, is not well done by environmental ignorance.

I would like to align myself with a heartfelt comment by biologist Michael Gough in a letter to Science concerning the efforts of veterans' groups and families to claim that soldiers in Vietnam got cancer because they were exposed to Agent Orange. Gough writes that:

> Agent Orange is one of the last vestiges of the nation's torment over the Vietnam War. Many members of Congress as well as many citizens are ashamed of our treatment of Vietnam veterans during and immediately after the war, a feeling that I share. But that guilt also fuels the continued search for evidence that Agent Orange "did" something to the health of veterans. It is ironic that the mental and emotional anguish caused by all wars is largely ignored while we search in vain for a chemical cause for diseases that occur as frequently in nonveterans as in veterans, and, so far as can be told, as frequently in veterans not exposed to Agent Orange as in those who were exposed. This is not the way to right any wrongs that may have been done.[57]

Exaggeration or worse for the right cause is the wrong way.

'Progressive' science

The journal *Science For the People*, which its sponsors describe correctly as progressive, devoted one of its 1989 issues exactly to this subject. The issue deserves a study of its own. Here I will merely quote from a single article by one Rick Hester, a pseudonym of a person who works for a state public health agency, and who writes about 'The Environmental Cancer Debate', the topic of the entire issue. Hester does not claim there is a cancer epidemic:

My reading of the cancer epidemiologic data is that there is still no convincing evidence for a chemically-induced cancer *epidemic* [emphasis in original] even though there are certain types that may be increasing in some areas because of historical exposures.

In his article he considers the views of Doll and Peto and the debate between Bruce Ames and Sam Epstein and Joel Schwartz, whose rebuttal to Ames was 'co-signed by a list which comprises a virtual "who's who" of progressive governmental scientists in the US'. Why, if it is science that is being discussed, are terms like 'progressive' appropriate? Hester turns to the area 'where the popular perception of cancer is most at odds with the mainstream scientific opinion'. In Woburn, Massachusetts, he notes, organised opinion was not against the much greater carcinogenic potency found in single mushrooms or in drinking wine but

the possibility that recklessly handled industrial solvents may have caused leukemia deaths in children. Whether Bruce Ames and his colleagues, or Richard Doll and his supporters in the scientific establishment like it or not, people are moved to act on what they perceive as "outrageous misconduct" by people who have put profit before the health and safety of their neighbours (or their workers).

And he concludes:

the overall import of our [the progressive scientists'] work has been to advance criticisms that expose the corporate greed at the root of many outrageous instances of excess cancer among workers or in the communities.

In his last sentence, Hester makes it clear that he will '...continue to critique the diversions and obfuscations of the scientific apologists for the multinational companies'.[58] What can be the fate of a science divided between 'progressives' and 'apologists'? Right before the reader's eyes, science gives way to ideology.

Who is there, I wonder, subjected to the barrage of negation, who does not believe that the physical environment is in terrible shape due to man-made, largely commercial development, while human health and safety is being assaulted for profit every second? That is a feat no paid propagandist could accomplish. Sincere propaganda can arise only by the willing subordination of judgement on behalf of a cause believed to be so profoundly good, whether called human equality or environmental purity, so that what begins as self-deception becomes societal delusion.[59]

Reliance on methodologies that give rise to the worst possible fears is a subject worthy of study in and of itself. How does one generate maximum fear?

Basic craft aspects of science are being disregarded. Control groups are not used; doctors are not called in to examine people who claim to be harmed; the 'double blind' procedure, in which the researchers would not know whose material they are examining, is not followed; even though it is known that a single study may produce wrong results, the required replication is not undertaken. Even within a single study, statistical outliers may drive policy.

When there are big differences between the phenomenon study and the subjects to which it is to be applied, eg mice and men, there have to be statistical models to apply the result from one to the other. If no such models exist or if there are many, all equally plausible, with no appropriate way of choosing among them, the task cannot be accomplished. Important as this extrapolation may be, no is no, for otherwise one is reduced either to choose at random or to prefigure the results. Know how is one thing, no can do another.

That laymen are prone to the kind of misrepresentations reported here is to be expected. When scientists are silent about scare talk using stock phrases like 'linked to cancer', however, that calls for some explanation. Are scientists reluctant to get involved in controversial matters? They seem to sign petitions often enough. Are they subject to sanctions? Personal abuse? Loss of funding? How? By whom? Do they believe what they do not contradict? If so, I am in grievous error and no further explanation is necessary. If they are unsure, perplexed, we need to understand why. What would they need to know to have firm opinions? Or has something happened at the heart of scientific disciplines to erode distinctions between what does (and does not) constitute evidence?

It is true that people who adhere to different cultures perceive different things to be safer or dangerous in widely varying ways.[60] But great differences in perception do not signify that all are equally in line with the evidence. Though each of us may perceive what we wish, we cannot necessarily make nature comply. Because much life and treasure are involved in conflicts over risk, it is worth trying to create more knowledge and more agreement on what counts as knowledge.

At every stage, from scaling in making estimates to the use of statistical models, the relation between industrial chemicals and human cancer has been vastly overestimated. While this tells us nothing about occupational exposures, it does tell us that this entire enterprise is so faulty it ought to be either severely revised or abolished. I speak here only of its basis in knowledge. In return I will undoubtedly be told that people's fears entering through the political system will not permit these changes to take place. My retort is that if the knowledge base is as faulty as has been presented here, so that it is misleading enough to be considered useless, and this view gains ground, it will make a lot of difference. I have yet to see or hear a public official who says that though there is no basis in fact for the fears at which certain legislation and regulation is aimed, he is going to support it anyway because the citizenry is too dumb to know otherwise. No enterprise can exist unless the people in it can make acceptable arguments to one another. Why don't we?

Notes and References

1. Marc Landy, 'Cleaning up Superfund', *The Public Interest*, no 85, Fall 1986, pp. 58-71.
2. Lewis Regenstein, *America the Poisoned*, Washington: Acropolis Books, 1982.
3. Tracy Freedman, 'Leftover Lives to Live,' *The Nation* May 23, 1981, pp. 624-627; Beverly Paigen, 'Health Problems in a Community Living Near the Hazardous Waste Site Known As Love Canal', paper presented at American Public Health Association Meeting, Detroit, Michigan, October 21, 1980.
4. American Medical Association news release, 'Love Canal Residents Not At Risk, Says CDC', March 16, 1984.
5. Adapted by the author from a 'Proposal for a Study of The Abuse of Science in Public Policy', by William R Havender, August 22, 1983.
6. *New York Times*, July 26, 1990, p.1.
7. *Science*, 27 April 1990, p.447.
8. Portney. See also John A Hird, 'Superfund Expenditures and Cleanup Priorities: Distributive Politics or the Public Interest?', *Journal of Policy Analysis and Management*, Vol 9, No 4, Fall 1990, pp. 455-483.
9. Leo Levenson, 'Unnecessary Risks', Graduate School of Public Policy, University of

California, Berkeley, December 6, 1989.

10. Ibid., p.9. Emphasis in original.

11. Ibid., p.10.

12. For background in risk assessment, see N C Lind, J S Nathwani, and E Siddall, *Managing Risks in the Public Interest*, Ontario: University of Waterloo Institute for Risk Research, 1991.

13. Frederick H Rueter and Wilbur A Steger, 'Air Toxics and Public Health: Exaggerating Risk and Misdirecting Policy', *Regulation*, Winter 1990, pp.51-60.

14. Ibid., pp.55-58.

15. I do not deal here with the adverse consequences for health of the decline in the standard of living caused by huge upward biases in risk estimates. For such a discussion, see my *Searching For Safety*, New Brunswick, NJ: Transaction Press, 1988. For critiques of this position and for my response, see *Society*, Vol.27, No.1, November/December 1989, pp.4-31.

16. Warren Brookes, 'Billions into the air-toxics breeze', *Washington Times*, January 17, 1990, pp.F1,F4.

17. Landy, 'Cleaning up Superfund', op cit. See also Michael A Kamrin and Paul W Rodgers (eds), *Dioxins in the Environment*, Washington DC: Heming Field, 1985.

18. Michael Gough, Director of the Centre of Risk Management at Resources for the Future, now with the Congressional Office of Technology Assessment, 'The Trials of Agent Orange', *Washington Times*, September 18, 1990, pp.G1,G4; and Peter Aleshire, 'Another Agent Orange Study', *Oakland Tribune*, October 20, 1990, p.C5. I have cited these newspaper pieces because they are written for general audiences.

19. Robert James Bidinotto, 'The Great Apple Scare', *Reader's Digest*, October 1990, pp.53-60.

20. Ibid.

21. Kenneth Smith, 'Alar: One Year Later, A Media Analysis of a Hypothetical Health Risk', *American Council on Science and Health*, March 1990, pp.1-9.

22. Bidinotto, 'Great Apple Scare', op cit.

23. Bruce N Ames and Lois Swirsky-Gold, Department of Biochemistry, University of California, Berkeley, and Cell Molecular Biology Division, Lawrence Berkeley Laboratory, 'Pesticides, Risk in Apple sauce', Letter to the Editor, *Science*, Vol.244, 19 May 1989, pp.755-57.

24. See the Op-Ed piece by chemist P J Wingate, *Baltimore Evening Sun*, October 11, 1989, 'All American Carcinogens', in which he argues that under conditions used for banning Alar, neither vanilla nor chocolate nor strawberry ice cream would make it. But why? 'Because vanilla ice cream contains vanillin, a carcinogen and potent poison with the chemical name of hydroxy methoxy benzaldehyde...'. Is pure vanilla a poison? 'It depends on the dose. A quarter of a spoonful of pure vanillin, either man-made or grown in a bean, would be a violent stomach poison and might cause cancer. Of course, no one ever takes even a hundredth of a spoonful of pure vanillin at one time - even if he or she eats a gallon of ice cream at a single sitting'.

25. See Michael Gough, 'How Much Cancer Can EPA Regulate Away?' *Risk Analysis*, Vol. 10, No. 1 (1990), pp. 1-6; and Maria Merritt, 'Alar: A Bad Apple?' typescript, Summer 1991, paper prepared for Aaron Wildavsky, University of California, Berkeley.

26. Christine F. Chaisson, 'Overview of the Evaluation of Carinogenic Risk of Daminozide and UDMH' Washington DC, Technical Assessment Systems, Inc, typescript, 1989, pp. 5, 13. Letter from Thomas H Jukes to Professor Richard Cellarius, October 5, 1990.

27. Bruce N Ames and Lois Swirsky Gold, 'Too Many Rodent Carcinogens: Mitogenesis increases Mutagenesis', *Science*, Vol.249, 31 August 1990, pp.970-71. See also their longer version, 'Chemical Carcinogenesis: Too many rodent carcinogens', *Proceedings of the National Academy of Sciences*, Vol.87, October 1990, pp.7772-76.

28. D A Freedman and H Zeisel, 'From Mouse to Man: The Quantitative Assessment of Cancer Risks', *Statistical Science*. P.7 of manuscript, Technical Report No.79, Dept. of Statistics, UCB, July 1, 1987.

29. Ibid., p.24.

30. Ibid., p.28.

31. Ibid.

32. Ibid., p.58. See also, for critical comments, Dean Marks, 'Animal Carcinogen Testing Challenge: Bruce Ames has stirred up the cancer research community by attacking one of the foundations of regulatory policy governing potential carcinogens', *Science*, Vol.250, 9 November 1990, pp.743-45. These comments vary from one that says that nobody knows what goes on at low doses, which may be true, but which does not meet the argument. Another is that a few rodent bioassays where a substance has shown to be cancerous also turn out to be cancerous in humans. But that is no better than asking for people's opinions on what hurts. Still others say that animal cancer tests may not be ideal but there is nothing to replace them. Again, nothing may be better than something if something is misleading. I should also add that Lester B Lave et al reported in *Nature* that 'Tests for human carcinogens using lifetime rodent bioassays are expensive, time-consuming and give uncertain results. For most chemicals such tests are not cost-effective'. Lester B Lave, Fanny K Ennever, Herbert S Rosenkranz, and Gilbert S Omenn, 'Information Value of the Rodent Bioassay', *Nature*, Vol.336, December 15, 1988, pp.631-33.

33. Michael Gough, 'How Much Cancer Can EPA Regulate Anyway?', *Risk Analysis*, Vol.10, No.1, 1990, p.1.

34. See also R Doll and R Peto, 'The Causes of Cancer: Quantitative Estimates of Avoidable Risks of Cancer in the United States Today', *Journal of the National Cancer Institute*, Vol.66, 1981, pp.113-138; and Michael Gough, 'Estimating Cancer Mortality: Epidemiological and Toxicological Methods Produce Similar Assessments', *Environmental Science and Technology*, Vol.23, August 1987, pp.925-30; and *Unfinished Business: A Comparative Assessment of Environmental Problems*, Washington, D.C., 1987, 'Carcinogenic Risk Assessments', Federal Register, Vol. 51, 1986, pp.3392-3403; and Office of Technology Assessment, Assessment of Technologies for Determining Cancer Risks From the Environment; EPA, *Unfinished Business: A Comparative Assessment of Environmental Problems*. Appendix 1: Report of the Cancer Risk Work Group, Washington, D.C., 1987.

35. Robert J Kalter et al, 'Biotechnology and the Dairy Industry: Production Costs and Commercial Potential of the Bovine Growth Hormone', Cornell University Center for Biotechnology, Ithaca, NY, December 1984, quoted in Geoffrey S Becker and Sarah Taylor, 'Bovine Growth Hormone (Somatotropin): Agricultural and Regulatory issues', Congressional Research Service, Library of Congress, November 20, 1986, p.2.

36. Bill Richards, 'Sour Reception Greets Milk Hormone', *Wall Street Journal*, September 15, 1989, p.B1.

37. Ibid.

38. See the statements by Jeremy Rifkin for the Foundation and Michael W Fox for the Humane Society before the Subcommittee on Livestock, Dairy, and Poultry of the Committee on Agriculture, 'Review of the Status and Potential Impact of Bovine

Growth Hormone', House of Representatives, June 11, 1986.

39. See D E Bauman, P J Eppard, M J DeGeeter, and G M Lanza, 'Responses of High Producing Dairy Cows to Long-Term Treatment with Pituitary-and-Recombinant Somatotropin', *Journal of Dairy Science*, Vol. 68, 1985, pp. 1352-1362.

40. Judith C Juskevich and C Greg Guyer, 'Bovine Growth Hormone: Human Food Safety Evaluation', Science, 24 August 1990,pp.875-883. Juskevich and Guyer worked for the Food and Drug Administration, Center for Veterinary Medicine, Office of New Animal Drug Evaluation, Division of Toxicology.

41. Ann Gibbons, 'FDA Publishes Bovine Growth Hormone Data', *Science*, Vol.249, 24 August 1990, pp.852-53.

42. William R Havender, 'EDB and the Marigold Option', *Regulation*, Vol 8, No 1, Jan/ Feb 1984, pp. 13-17.
   The story of DES (diethylstilbestrol), used to produce more and leaner meat from sheep and cattle, is similar to the ones I have reported. There the comparison is between five nanograms of DES and those who, for medicinal purposes, which led to abortions, received 50 nanograms a day for 35 weeks. See Thomas H Jukes, 'Carcinogenicity of Female Sex Hormones, Especially as Related to Use in Pregnancy and in Meat Production', in G H Gass and H M Kaplan, (eds) *CRC Handbook of Endocrinology*, Vol.2, Part B, Boca Raton, Fl: CRC Press, 1987, pp143-58.

43. 'Agency Admits EDB Threat was Overestimated', reprinted in *Farmer's Exchange*, May 4, 1984.

44. Sorell L Schwartz, letter to the Editor, *Regulation*, June 28, 1984.

45. The original study was Irving J Selikoff, Jacob Churg, and Cuyler E Hammond, 'Asbestos exposure and neoplacia', *Journal of the American Medical Association*, Vol.188, 1964, pp.22-26.

46. William Booth, 'Risk of One Type of Asbestos Discounted', *Washington Post*, January 19, 1990, p.A8. See also the article in the *New York Times* by William K Stevens, 'Despite Asbestos Risk, Experts See No Cause for "Fiber Phobia"', September 5, 1989, p.C4. This article gives pictures of different types of asbestos with a subtitle, 'Asbestos Danger Varies By Type'.

47. Michael Fumento, 'The Asbestos Rip-Off', *American Spectator*, October 1989, pp.21-26.

48. Ibid.

49. *New England Journal of Medicine*, June 28, 1989. The best article on this subject for the layman is by Donald N Dewees, 'Does the danger from asbestos in buildings warrant the cost of taking it out?' *American Scientist*, Vol.75 (May-June 1987), pp.285-88. Dewees is professor of law and economics at the University of Toronto with a BS degree in electrical engineering. He was Director of Research for the Ontario Royal Commission on Asbestos, and also a Gilbert White fellow at Resources for the Future in Washington, D C, where he wrote *Controlling Asbestos in Buildings*, Resources for the Future, 1986. His conclusion is that 'Furthermore, removal shifts risks from building occupants and maintenance workers to removal workers. Yet despite the many variations, one conclusion seems reasonably clear: we should resist squandering our resources on crash programs of asbestos removal to reduce already insignificant risks lest we find ourselves unprepared to cope with more acute risks from other hazards or even from the programs themselves' (p.288).

50. B T Mossman et al, 'Asbestos: Scientific Developments and Implications for Public Policy', *Science*, Vol.247, 19 January, 1990, pp.294-300; quote on p.299.

51. See Malcolm Ross, US Geological Survey, 'Minerals and Health: The Asbestos

Problem', *Proceedings of the 21st Forum on the Geology of Industrial Minerals*, edited by H Wesley Peirce, special paper no.4, 1987, pp.83-89.

52. Of course, the controversy is not over. For a representative sample of thrust and counter-thrust, see the objections to the Mossman and Gee article and their response in *Science*, Vol.248, May 1990, pp.795-802.

53. Mossman and Gee, 'Asbestos: Scientific Developments...' op cit. See also the interesting exchange of letters from Dr Bernard Goldstein, MD, Assistant Administrator for Research and Development, to Malcolm Ross, dated January 11, 1985, asking Ross to review a paper that seemed to Goldstein to suggest an excess of mesotheliomas in the white asbestos industry; Ross's reply of February 28, 1985; the author of the paper in question, Dr Andrew Churg's reply of March 18, 1985 that though he had some minor disagreements 'On the whole I agree with you that any attempt to use this paper as a reason for removing chrysotile asbestos from schools or other public buildings has no scientific basis whatsoever'; and the review of this exchange by Professor J Corbett McDonald, MP FRCP of the School of Occupational Health, McGill University to the effect that '...one gets rather tired of having scientific studies misinterpreted'. This exchange is available from Mr Ross at the Geological Survey.

54. Ibid., p.299.

55. Irving J Selikoff and Douglas H K Lee with Harry Anderson et al, Asbestos and Disease, New York: Academic Press, 1978; Irving J Selikoff and E Cuyler Hammond, (eds), *Health Hazards of Asbestos Exposure*, New York Academy of Sciences, 1979.

56. Andrew C Revkin, 'Special Report Endless Summer: Living with the Greenhouse Effect', *Discover*, October 1988, pp 50-61.

57. *Science*, Vol.245, 8 September 1989, p.1031, by Michael Gough, then with Resource for the Future, now with the congressional Office of Technological Assessment.

58. Rick Hester, 'The Environmental Cancer Debate', *Science for the People*, Vol.21, No.1, 1989, pp.9-11.

59. See Mary Douglas and Aaron Wildavsky, *Risk and Culture*, University of California Press, 1982; Karl Dake and Aaron Wildavsky, 'Theories of Risk Perception: Who Fears What and Why?' *Daedalus*, Vol.119, No.4, Fall 1990, pp.41-60; and Michael Thompson and Aaron Wildavsky, 'A Proposal to Create a Cultural Theory of Risk', in H C Kunreuther and Engl V Ley (eds.), *The Risk Analysis Controversy: An Institutional Perspective*, Berlin: Springer-Verlag, 1983.

60. See Dake and Wildavsky, 'Theories of Risk Perception', *Daedalus*, op cit.

11   The Good Life and the New Class

Irving Kristol

The public health debate is in part a class war

I propose here to discuss the good life. This is a nice simple issue, and is the main battlefield in what I can only describe as a class war - a war between those who believe in the good life and those who believe in the better life, or those who believe that the good life is not good enough.

What do we mean by the good life? It's an ordinary conception, a common person's perception of the good life: health and prosperity - these are regarded as the prerequisites of a good life. Everyone understands that these don't necessarily guarantee a happy life. Happiness is something else entirely. But a good life is a life of health and prosperity.

We have, however - and have had for almost two centuries now - a lot of people who think that this good life which finds its expression in a capitalist economy and a bourgeois society is not good enough; that it needs to be replaced, or at least stretched, to include a better life. They find this conception of the good life, which most ordinary people are content with - though, as I shall indicate, this may be changing - not good enough. Or they simply hold it in contempt, along with the whole modern world and its science and technology.

The modern reaction against science

I often hear astonishment expressed that people should be against science and technology, in view of all the good that they have achieved. Well, these people want all the good achievements, or some of them. They just don't want the science and technology that produce them. You don't have to read the deep thinkers. You don't have to read the German philosophers, like Heidegger, who attack modernity as the debasement of humanity. Read science fiction, which is what our children are reading. If you look at science fiction over the past 50 years, what is its message? Its message is anti-scientific and anti-technological. It is all horror stories of how science and technology dehumanise the human race and result in terrible tyrannies. That strain of thought has been with us for close on 200 years and has always been influential among a small class of writers and thinkers. On left and on right, it doesn't really matter.

Back in 1900, in Germany, the first youth and environmentalist movement was formed. It was mainly on the Right. Many of its members went camping in the mountains to be close to nature; they despised modern amenities. They were not boy scouts and many of them ended up in the Nazi youth movement. The Social Democrats tried to compete by forming their own youth movement, but were unable to divorce themselves from rationality in so radical a way. It was not a fair competition.

This impulse is very old, and it is worth asking why it has now become so powerful, and especially so since the 1960s. I think the answer lies in the one word - affluence.

The unexpected consequences of affluence

An affluent society - and ours is the first in history - is one of which we have no experience. It turns out to be full of surprises. I think it was John Adams who said that we devote our lives to commerce and war so that our grandchildren can cultivate the arts. Well, it's not his grandchildren, but his great, great grandchildren; and they don't cultivate the arts: they cultivate power. He did not foresee that. But none of us, I think, could have foreseen it.

Affluence has a power of its own which we are only beginning to recognise. We see this as parents in terms of youth culture - the pop culture of young people, hard rock, Madonna, rap records, whatever; these are things that most adults of my own age are not comfortable with.

Youth culture funded by indulgent, uncomprehending parents

How did this happen? Where did this particular youth culture come from? I know where it came from: it came from youth pockets. It came from money. For the first time, young people have had the power to create their own culture because they have the money to pay for it. By the late 1950s, they had taken over the record industry, which, apart from its small classical market, was now catering almost entirely to the newly-affluent young. Records were not that cheap, but this was the first generation of young people which had economic power of its own, and was able to exercise it without parental supervision. What were parents to do? Were they to start examining every record, and draw up a forbidden list? Some parents have done just that. It's not a bad idea, but is demanding on parents who have much else to worry about.

During the 1960s, the young took over the movie industry. I mean this as a matter of economic statistics. The industry suddenly began turning out films for young people. This had not previously been the case. How did it happen? The young bought the movie industry with money that their parents had given them. For this reason, it was so difficult to talk about censorship or call for government involvement, when those who were buying pornography and obscenity were doing so in the free market.

A new class has been created by affluence

Affluence has also given birth to what has been called the New Class. This is a vague term, and no useful purpose is served by trying to give it too precise a meaning. But one recognises its members when one sees them.

The New Class comprises a minority - not a large one - of a certain generation, which is ambitious, bright, on the whole enterprising, often bold. Its members were born into upper middle class families. I recall the wonderful saying coined by the young man who led the 1960s student revolt at Columbia - Mark Rudd - it became the title of a New York Magazine article: 'You Don't Know What Hell is Like Unless You Were Raised in Scarsdale'.

Of course, the whole ambition of ordinary people, and the whole purpose of a market economy and bourgeois society is to let everyone live in places like Scarsdale. That is what we are good at creating. That is what we have created. But these young people don't want to live in Scarsdale. They aren't interested in going into business, or even in making money. What they are interested in is imposing themselves on the world. They want power. There are no military careers open to them, no wars or empires for them to throw themselves into. Instead, they must stay at home and order us around. They aren't all socialists. Many who do call themselves socialist don't know what they mean by the word. They don't want to run things, but people. They want to run the people who run the corporations. Today, they are doing this rather well.

The march through the institutions

This New Class has emerged from affluence unexpectedly. Its members are the grandchildren that John Adams was talking about. But it turns out they don't want to sit around and look at paintings and play in quartets and do all the other things he hoped they would. They do want to 'participate', and they're clever enough to know that they are a minority, so there's no point in their getting directly involved in politics for the most part. Some do, but most of them do not. That would not be a very smart thing to do: they could lose an election. What they have done is engage in what a Marxist called - though with something else in mind - the 'march through the institutions'.

They begin by getting control of our universities. Once upon a time, these were full of fuddy duddy professors. I remember such times. At Oxford in England, modern history ended in 1789. Nothing dealing with a later period than that was taught: that was journalism. In my own day at City College, I recall, there was not a single course in the literature department on contemporary literature, or what we would call modern literature. You couldn't take a course on Joyce, or Mann, Kafka, Faulkner, or F.Scott Fitzgerald. No one thought it was right to study these in the university. You read Spencer's *Faerie Queene* and Chaucer and Shakespeare and Milton. This is why I never majored in English.

But that fuddy duddy university which really did regard itself as a kind of ivory tower - and a place which preserved pre-capitalist and pre-bourgeois traditions to elevate the individual as he would not be elevated through participation in a commercial society - vanished in the 1950s and 1960s as a result, again, of affluence. Counting community colleges, there was one university campus being established in the United States every day during the late 1950s and early 1960s. Who was to staff them? Young people were. They moved into the universities and captured control of academia, which control they have held ever since.

In the same way, they moved into journalism. This had always been a low grade profession. Prior to the end of the Second World War, it was very rare to find a journalist who had ever been to college. I recall some of the best of these old guys - Scotty Reston, for example. I doubt if any of them had a college degree, and they were the cream of the crop. That changed as college graduates began to move into journalism, to create what we today call the media, and to set themselves up as a competing power to government. This they have done very effectively. I doubt if people realise just how effectively the media have become a competitive power to government. I'm living now in Washington DC, and I know how frustrated people in government are by the fact that their boss, who might be a Cabinet Secretary, can make what seems an important statement on some matter that doesn't even get reported. No one is interested. The media will have decided that it isn't a story. They decide what to report and what not to report, and how to report it.

The New Class is now in control of those who control society

And so these people have taken over both academia and the media. They also have the law and divinity schools, so that they now produce the new lawyers and clerics. I may be talking only about a minority, but it's a very ambitious, intelligent and vigorous minority. They have complete control over the higher educational system, and they use this to try to remake the whole social order.

I doubt if they have any clear idea of what they want. In fact, I know they don't have one. What they are clear on is that they would run the country better than the people running it now. After all, they reason, many of them have PhDs. Where's the point of having one of these if you can't think yourself better at running the country than the guy who hasn't got one? Education counts for something, surely?

The New Class seeks, and is expected, to banish worries that are caused by affluence

As a result, the new Class wants to run things. In wanting this, it is both post-capitalist and post-socialist. It's certainly collectivist and statist. But it is all this in quite a new and unfamiliar way - a way very difficult to cope with.

Another problem of affluence is that it creates hypochondria. The more affluent people are, the more hypochondriacal they are. Poor people are stoical, or so they used to be. Before the Second Word War, they were stoical. They got sick. They died. There wasn't much to be done. It wasn't even inability to afford medical treatment, for that had its limits. People died and they were buried; and that was that. But the more affluent people are, the more entitled they feel to health. I think that's human nature. But, in a more affluent society, people will be more unreasonably demanding that somehow or other government, or whatever institution or institutions are involved, will address their health problems - will address them and solve them.

And the New Class is the problem-solving class. It may not, in fact, solve any of the problems, but that is its claim to authority. Eventually, it will become clear to it that it cannot solve them. Of what will happen then, I confess I have no idea. That will be a new world. But, for the moment, we're stuck with that class to which we have - often literally - given birth.

The new paganism

It has taken over, to some degree, some of the anti-bourgeois, anti-modern impulses of the 19th and early 20th centuries. Its members think it's wrong to be stoical. They tend, some of them, to be secular. But there are religious spin-offs from the New Class. One of these can fairly be described as the new paganism. The religious impulse doesn't die, instead, in the New Class, or in its children - for they too have children and face the problems that parents have always faced - are neo-pagans who invent new religions on the spot. These usually involve Mother Nature and are associated with extreme environmentalism.

I don't know how many people noticed the editorial published in the *New York Times* on Mother's Day in 1991. Not many people read the *New York Times*, thank goodness. But this was the third editorial, relatively short. It described a neo-pagan ceremony in Central Park. It described how a group of around 40 young people - some not so young - stood around looking at bowls of water, communing with a tree, and uttering an invented prayer to Mother Nature. And the editorial approved, saying it was appropriate on Mother's Day to give a prayer for Mother Nature! Mother's Day was not invented with this sort of thing in mind. But that is now what is with us, if not always in so extreme a form. If the *New York Times* can accept this quasi-religious extreme of the environmentalist movement, I guess we're stuck with it for a while.

Conclusion

So, I think we have some deep problems. It's not just a question of educating the people: who's going to do the educating? We can educate a few, but since the activists control the universities -by now, the high schools as well - it's not so easy to educate large numbers of people. I think we are fighting a defensive action, a holding action. Our advantage is that they cannot succeed in governing in a way that will satisfy ordinary men and women, which is why so many of them are against a free society. On the other hand, there they are. The laws have been passed, the institutions set up, the rules made: and I think our experience of the past ten years under quite conservative administrations indicates the difficulty of rolling back the wave.

I think we are fighting a holding battle. It's a great battle to fight. I've been fighting it now for 25 years, and I encourage others to join. It's a lot of fun. I will not pretend that winning would not be more fun - but I don't see that happening in the very near future.

Manhattan Institute

The Social Affairs Unit

The Unit is a research and educational trust, established in 1980 and committed to the promotion of lively and wide-ranging debate on social affairs. Its authors – now numbering well over 100 – have analysed the factors which make for a free and orderly society in which enterprise can flourish. Major recent studies from the Unit include: *A Diet of Reason*; *Sense and Nonsense in the Healthy Eating Debate*; *Drinking to your Health: the Allegations and the Evidence*; *The Megaphone Solution: Government attempts to cure social problems through mass media campaigns*; *The Secret of the Miracle Economy: different national attitudes to competitiveness and money*; *Cradle to Grave: comparative perspectives on the state of welfare*; *Educational Achievement in Japan: lessons for the west*; *Full Circle: bringing up children in the post-permissive society*; *Advertising Bans: administrative decisions or matters of principle?* and *Advertising Bans: consequences for consumers*. The Unit's work is overseen by a Board of Trustees and assisted by an Academic Advisory Council. To maintain its independence, the SAU is funded by a wide range of foundations and trusts, sales of its publications and corporate subscriptions from highly diverse sectors. The Social Affairs Unit is registered as an educational charity in the UK, charity number 281530.

5th Floor
30 Old Burlington Street
London W1X 1LB
England
Tel: 071 287 2297